*Recipes
For
A Good
Life*

VEGAN & GLUTEN FREE

Recipes For A Good Life

―◆―

JOANINHA

REGENT PRESS
Berkeley, California

Copyright © 2025 by Joaninha

Paperback
ISBN 13: 978-1-58790-678-7
ISBN 10: 1-58790-678-3

Hardback
ISBN 13: 978-1-58790-679-4
ISBN 10: 1-58790-679-1

Library of Congress Control Number: 2024905232

DISCLAIMER

The recommendations in this book are based on the author's education and personal experience. The dietary guidelines herein are not to be considered as a substitute for consultation with a licensed physician or health practitioner.

PRINTED IN THE U.S.A.
REGENT PRESS
Berkeley, California
www.regentpress.net

Contents

Introduction

Part One: Health Basics
- Love Your Body and Mother Earth 11
- Lifestyle Matters More Than Genes 12
- The Microbiome — Our Key To Vibrant Health 14
- Balance Acid-Forming & Alkaline-Forming Foods 16
- Feel Your Best Every Day — Practice a Healthy Lifestyle 17
- Exercise & Detoxify 18
- Get the Most From What You Eat 20

Part Two: Additional Recommendations
- Cook to Thrive 21
- Mealtime Mindfulness 22
- Culinary Mastery 26
- Eat the Freshest Foods For Utmost Vitality 28
- Fortify Your Body with Essential Fatty Acids 31
- Beneficial Oils & Fats 32
- Liberate Yourself from Sugar 38
- Replace Anti-Nutrient Foods with Nutrient-Rich Alternatives 46
- Gluten-Free Whole Grains 47
- Have Fun with Herbs & Spices 53
- Self-Healing Medicinal Spices 61

Part Three: Recipes

14 Menu Plans 69

Timing & Cooking Methods 85

Healing Beverages 95

Breakfasts 107

Snacks & Appetizers 119

Soups 131

Salads 145

Main Dishes 157

Vegetable Sides 177

Desserts 191

Dressings, Sauces, Condiments 199

Part Four: Resources

How-to Basics 219

Ingredient Glossary 222

Bibliography 234

Appendix 235

Index 239

Acknowledgements 247

About the Author 248

INTRODUCTION

The idea for *Recipes For A Good Life* was born while I was living in France. I worked as a dietary consultant, gave cooking classes, and wrote articles for the "Riviera Insider." My clients loved my food and benefited from my advice, so they kept telling me I should write a cookbook. Their enthusiasm motivated me to begin.

How To Use This Book

My recommendation is to start with what resonates most with you and make changes gradually. As you experience having more energy, you will feel naturally motivated to do more to care for yourself. The guidelines are described simply so they are easy to follow and integrate into your life.

By adopting these guidelines you will learn how to:

- Establish habits for radiant health
- Get the most nutrition from what you eat
- Lower your risk of degenerative disease

Part One
Health Basics

These chapters acquaint you with beneficial foods and good eating habits.

Part Two
Additional Recommendations

This section emphasizes selecting the freshest foods, cooking for yourself, consuming essential fatty acids, and phasing sugar out.

Part Three
Recipes

Here you can put into practice what you learned in Parts One and Two. You can experiment with menu plans and different cooking methods. Plus create truly nourishing, satisfying meals from the collection of recipes.

Part Four
Resources

Basic preparation techniques and a glossary of ingredients are featured here.

Informative sidebars throughout the book feature personal stories, time saving tips, and interviews with an organic farmer, an olive oil producer, and a bee keeper.

A Lifelong Search
For Natural Pathways to Wellness

This cookbook is the result of a lifetime of searching for effective ways to enhance healing. My interest in diet and nutrition began at an early age. In childhood, I caught colds easily and suffered from ailments that sometimes sent me to the hospital. After a ten-day stay in the hospital at age 14, I returned to school feeling weak and weighing only 90 pounds. My desire to gain weight and feel stronger motivated me to find my own way to better health.

I began by reading about diet and exercise, and discovered that carbohydrates and protein could help me gain weight. Upon high school graduation, I was eager to learn more so I decided to study Home Economics to specialize in foods and nutrition. The program taught dietary planning, meal preparation techniques, and methods of efficiency. This developed a new interest for me in meal planning and food preparation.

One day I saw a flyer for a hatha yoga class on a campus bulletin board. Always looking for ways to improve, I signed up. The instructor recommended vegetarianism so I gave it a try. By eliminating meat, I no longer felt drowsy after meals and had more energy than ever, leading me to become a vegetarian. The remarkable results I was enjoying led me to pursue alternative holistic remedies.

Feeling that direct experience was my best teacher, I decided to go to South America to study about the properties of healing plants. After graduation, I made my way to the municipality of Sibundoy in Colombia. There, I was welcomed by a native healer as a member of his family with whom I stayed for eight weeks.

One night I experienced an intense abdominal pain so sharp I could hardly move. My moans awakened the family and they motioned me to sit outside in back of their grass home. The healer crushed some dried herbs and spread them over me while chanting in his language. This lasted about 3 to 4 minutes. When his chanting stopped, the pain disappeared and I fell into a deep sleep. Before this night he had spoken to me about the healing spirits in plants. What I witnessed was living proof of the healing power of plants, and it has left a lasting impression on me.

Next, I decided to study traditional diets

known for their longevity attributes in Japan and the Mediterranean. Living in these places, I saw a direct relationship between my vitality and eating locally grown, seasonal foods. Eating this way helped my body adjust to the changing weather patterns. In Japan, for example, hot miso soups and stews with root vegetables are served in winter to warm the body, while cooked dishes and beverages are served at room temperature in summer to give relief from heat and humidity.

Observing the effects traditional diets have had on my body has convinced me that the healthiest people do not have to count calories or avoid carbohydrates. They eat simple meals made with ingredients fresh from the garden, a neighboring farm, or the sea. And they live in harmony with nature.

The next chapter of my search came when I was given a copy of *The Perfect Health* by Deepak Chopra. This opened my eyes to an approach that I'd never thought of—tailoring diet to balance the individual's constitution. This made so much sense to me, bringing together all that I had previously learned. A questionnaire in the book helped me identify my constitutional type and plan my diet accordingly.

To delve deeper I scheduled a consultation with an Ayurvedic practitioner. She made several recommendations that were unfamiliar and seemed awkward at first. Once established, they became a natural part of my routine resulting in a harmonious balance within. That was 20 years ago, and the longer I practice the greater the benefits become. I continue to research through an array of works by Ayurvedic masters such as Dr. Vasant Lad and Dr. Robert Svoboda.

This book presents a synthesis of the dietary principles I have integrated from a variety of systems over a lifetime of experimentation. Now I rarely fall prey to illness and my recuperative response is swift. Once, I fractured the radial bone in my left arm and it healed so quickly that the osteopath threw the cast away, proclaiming, "Your bone has mended itself." Relying on ancient knowledge and traditional wisdom, I have learned how to use food and natural remedies to cure my body.

I am sharing my personal story to acquaint you with the many discoveries I made, as illness motivated me to seek holistic alternatives and guided me to a more conscious way of living. Through my life's experiences I have learned firsthand the power of the body to heal itself.

Be your body's best friend. The power to heal yourself is within you. Lift your spirits and rejoice!

AYURVEDA
ANCIENT WAYS OF NATURAL HEALING

Derived from the Indian books of wisdom known as the Vedas, Ayurveda plays a complementary role with yoga in promoting physical well-being and spiritual evolution. This 5,000-year-old holistic system is the mother of all other medical systems, including Chinese and Western medicines. In Sanskrit, *ayur* means "life" or "lifespan," and *veda* means "knowledge" or "science." Its principles and practices are based on the five elements of nature: space, air, fire, water, and earth. Combinations of these elements make up three life energies known as *doshas*: 1) *vata* (movement), a combination of air and space; 2) *pitta* (transformation), a combination of fire and water; and 3) *kapha* (stability), a combination of water and earth. These energetic forces manifest differently in each individual. The ratios in which these *doshas* are present give each person his or her unique physical, mental, behavioral, and spiritual qualities.

According to Ayurveda, disease and illness result from an imbalance of the three *doshas*. Therefore, Ayurvedic recommendations focus on balancing the *doshas* using an individualized approach to healing that evaluates each person's unique nature and how it is influenced by lifestyle, nutrition, climate, and environment.

Integrating a few basic Ayurvedic principles into one's life can result in profound healing. The goal of Ayurveda is to restore a harmonious balance to the individual in support of longevity. With simple changes in diet and daily routine, Ayurvedic therapies have helped people improve their health around the globe. To learn more, contact the Ayurvedic Institute at

www.ayurveda.com

Love Your Body & Mother Earth

Examining our food preferences and eating habits can give us a deeper understanding of how well we nurture our body and our planet. Often without realizing it, instead of making our own well-being a priority, we devote more time and energy to caring for family members, advancing in our careers, and seeking diversions. Yet our bodies are invigorated when we give ourselves loving attention and honor our physical needs. How to achieve this is simple. When hungry, eat nutritious food. When thirsty, drink filtered water. When tired, take rest. You may even find that treating your body with respect will help condition you to treat others with more consideration as well.

The power of choice is one of our greatest gifts. Making conscious food choices is an act of self-love that impacts our quality of life and the health of our planet. Think about these questions:

- Does the food I eat give me the energy and essential nutrients I need?
- Do my food choices preserve biodiversity and keep soil and water toxin free?
- Do my eating habits support kind treatment of animals?

Lifestyle Matters More Than Genes

Research confirms that diet and lifestyle are more influential than the genes we inherit in determining our vulnerability to disease. This is because genes can be stimulated or suppressed depending on what we consume and how we live. Scientific studies now link disease to poor diet and eating habits; and physicians are beginning to consider the condition of the gut in analyzing a patient's health, even if there are no digestive complaints.

Our food choices are the essence of disease prevention and a primary mode of treatment. For these reasons, it's wise to select foods that provide essential nutrients and keep our bodies from accumulating toxins. Foods that are plentiful in antioxidants and phytochemicals can minimize the consequences of exposure to health-compromising toxins. Try some of these recommendations to boost your immunity:

- Consume dark leafy greens and colorful vegetables in abundance. The deeper the color, the richer in vitamins and minerals.
- Make cruciferous vegetables dietary staples as they contain compounds that help to prevent cancer. Cabbage, bok choy, Brussels sprouts, cauliflower, and broccoli are some examples.
- Enjoy root vegetables such as beets, carrots, yams, and sweet potatoes often.
- Buy fresh locally-grown, seasonal produce. Shop at farmers markets. Plant a garden! Grow herbs on the windowsill to garnish and add flavor to meals.
- Select organic ingredients and leave skins on for an antioxidant booste. Fruits and vegetables protect themselves from predators with the antioxidants in their skins. Their nutrients are most plentiful in or just beneath their skins.

- Eat fermented foods daily to promote the growth of beneficial microorganisms in the intestines. Fermented foods are one of the best sources of beneficial bacteria and probiotics. The more variety of fermented foods the greater the benefit. About 1 tablespoon a day is sufficient. Consistent consumption is most important.
- Use spices and seasonings generously in cooking. They are nutrient dense while they also make food tastier.

How the Body Responds to Dietary Changes

Once you decide to quit eating processed foods and to replace them with more nutrient-dense alternatives such as those recommended in this book, you may initially experience discomfort in the form of fatigue, headaches, digestive uneasiness, skin rashes, or even anxiety and depression. If this happens, be patient and take heart in knowing that these changes are simply a sign that toxins are being released from your system. These unpleasant symptoms should disappear within a few days.

The good news is that once your new eating habits are established, the results will be significant and lasting. You will feel stronger and younger every day, so celebrate that a new zest for life will soon be yours!

The Microbiome
Our Key To Vibrant Health

The microorganisms that live in the digestive tract of humans and other animals is known as the microbiome.

Our intestinal flora are responsible for a multitude of functions. These microbes enhance the immune system, maintain healthy intestinal cells, digest carbohydrates, and are responsible for energy storage and more. In short, beneficial bacteria are our friends!

A high consumption of sugar, processed foods, alcohol, and doses of antibiotics can upset the balance of our intestinal flora and increase the growth of pathogenic bacteria and yeast. Replacing the intake of these less than nutritional foods, beverages, and medications with good eating habits (page 20) can make a significant difference in how well we feel.

To promote the growth of healthy gut bacteria, eat foods that feed beneficial bacteria. Eating fermented foods along with a diet high in fiber can help favorable organisms flourish in the digestive tract. Three dietary habits to adopt:

- Eat a wide variety of fermented foods.
- Have a fermented food every day.
- Make fiber-rich foods a dietary staple.

Fermented Foods

Fermentation to preserve foods has been used by traditional cultures for centuries. Today we can employ this timeless wisdom to improve digestion and the absorption of nutrients by including fermented foods in our daily diet. The wider the variety, the more diverse our microbial community will be. Here are some you can choose from:

- Coconut yogurt
- Crème fraîche
- Kefir
- Kimchi
- Miso
- Natto (fermented soybeans)
- Pickled cucumbers
- Pickled ginger (page 220)
- Sauerkraut
- Yogurt

Ways to Boost Your Intake

- Go Japanese with a cup of miso broth instead of tea or coffee with breakfast. Add 1 to 2 teaspoons miso paste to 1 cup (8 fl oz/250 ml) boiled water.
- Flavor soups and stews with miso. (Miso Barley Soup, page 138-139)
- Make a delicious marinade for veggies. (Baked Parsnips in Miso-Almond Butter Sauce, page 186)
- 30 to 40 minutes after lunch have an Indian lassi. (pages 103 & 104)
- Serve a tablespoon of fermented vegetables or raw sauerkraut as a condiment with meals.

Balance Acid-Forming & Alkaline-Forming Foods

A vital prerequisite for managing our health is maintaining the proper alkaline balance. When we are well our body temperature is 98.6°F (37°C), and when it goes up, it is a sign of illness. In the same way, a fluctuation of the blood pH indicates an imbalance in the body—the first phase of disease before any symptoms appear.

To maintain the proper pH balance both acid- and alkaline-forming foods are necessary. Consuming a ratio of 80% alkaline-forming foods to 20% acid-forming foods can keep us functioning at our best.

Alkaline-Forming Foods

A diet plentiful in alkaline-forming foods makes good sense. Vegetables are the largest alkaline-forming food group, so eating 4+ cups (about 1 pound/500g) of vegetables daily can keep our blood pH on the alkaline side. (See Appendix page 236-237 for a list of alkaline-forming foods)

Acid-Forming Foods

All foods become more acidic when sugar is added. Food heated in a microwave may also contribute to the acidic content of the blood. Mental and physical stresses, as well as allergic reactions, can move our blood pH to the acidic side. (See Appendix page 235 for a list of acid-forming foods)

Note: The glycemic index (GI) measures how quickly blood sugar rises after consumption of a carbohydrate-containing food, using a scale that ranges from 0-100. Acid-forming foods generally rate on the 50+ side. Simple carbohydrates rate the highest with white sugar scoring 100.

You can learn more in *The pH Miracle* (see the bibliography, page 234).

Feel Your Best Every Day

Practice a Healthy Lifestyle

Select fresh, organic, seasonal ingredients

Eat vegetables in abundance

Consume essential fatty acids daily

Keep intake of sweets to a minmum

Enjoy home cooking more, eat out less

Infuse the food you prepare with love

Focus on what you're eating, avoid distraction

Adopt regular detoxification practices

Get plenty of fresh air, exercise, and rest

Exercise & Detoxify

Exercise Regularly

- Improve circulation
- Flush the lymph system
- Tone muscles
- Burn fat
- Support detoxification

Stay fit and keep the mind calm with twenty to sixty minutes of exercise five to six times per week. Yoga and walking are excellent.

Move! When sitting at your computer or watching TV, stand up every 20 minutes, stretch, walk across the floor or dance in place before sitting back down. This can prevent stiffness and alleviate pain.

Keep a cheerful attitude! Studies have shown that optimism strengthens the body's immune system and reduces stress. Practicing gratitude and forgiveness has been shown to support wellness.

Take time for self-reflection every day. Meditate. Spend time in nature to strengthen your connection with your inner self.

Detoxify

Prevent an accumulation of toxins by adopting detoxification practices as a regular part of your routine.

Morning Cleanse

Stimulate the release of toxins by using a tongue scraper upon arising. The less the tongue is coated, the more flavorful food will taste. A coated tongue indicates a build-up of toxins in the body.

Clear toxins by swishing a tablespoon of sesame or coconut oil in the mouth for 10 to 15 minutes after tongue scraping. To avoid clogging plumbing, spit it into the toilet or the trash and then rinse the mouth with warm salt water. This is an Ayurvedic practice known as *oil pulling*.

After tongue scraping and oil pulling, drink a cup of hot water with 1/2 teaspoon of lemon or lime juice or apple cider vinegar, or have a cup of herbal tea. (See Healing Beverages, page 95)

Massage

This soothing form of bodywork boosts oxygen supply, increases blood and lymph flow, and balances the nervous system.

Saunas and Steam Baths

These ancient methods of cleansing and purification relax the body and mind. When we sweat profusely, the skin transforms oil-based toxins into water-based ones that are flushed out through the pores.

Natural Thermal Hot Springs

Soaking in mineral waters can help eliminate toxins, relieve pain, and offer deep relaxation.

Detox Baths at Home

Baths are a simple way to release stored toxins from the body. They are expecially effective after massages, acupuncture, fasting, and aerobic exercise.

To remove heavy metals and chemicals, add this combination to a hot bath:

- 1 cup of Apple Cider Vinegar
- 1 cup of Epsom salt (Magnesium Sulfate)
- 2 bottles (32 oz each) of 3% hydrogen peroxide

Soak in the bath for 20 minutes. Enjoy.

Note: Add 1 cup baking soda to draw out radiation from x-rays, cell phone towers, computer screens, and televisions.

To balance PH and help treat fungal infections, add this formula to a hot bath.:

- 1 cup Borax
- 1 cup baking soda (sodium bicarbonate)
- 2 bottles (32 oz each) of 3% hydrogen peroxide

Luxuriate in the bath for 20 minutes.

Note: Fresh sprigs of rosemary and essential oils, such as lavender, or sea salt may be added to pull additional toxins from the body.

Get the Most From What You Eat

Good eating habits can enhance our digestion, boost our immune system, and reduce the production of toxins in our body. Follow these recommendations consistently for optimal results.

- Eat because you're hungry, not because you're bored, depressed, or want something to do.

- Sit down to eat and give your full attention to what you're eating. Refrain from watching television, reading, working, and using electronic devices until after your meal.

- Chew your food well. Notice the pleasurable sensations of flavors and textures that will activate proper digestive enzymes.

- Drink room-temperature water between meals to stay hydrated. Having liquids with meals dilutes digestive juices. Iced beverages and cold drinks are not recommended as they hamper digestion and can cause the formation of toxins.

- Leave three to four hours between meals to allow the body to complete the digestive process. For deeper sleep, finish dinner at least three hours before bedtime. The greater the number of hours between dinner and breakfast, the more time the body has for detoxification and healing.

- Eat until hunger is satisfied. Your stomach needs room to process ingested food, so avoid overeating.

- Buy the freshest seasonal, locally grown, produce you can find. Shop at farmers markets. Plant a vegetable and herb garden.

- Prepare your own meals. The more often you cook for yourself, the healthier you will be!

- Use conventional cooking methods rather than relying on a microwave oven.

- Eat meals at the same time every day. The body functions best with a regular routine.

COOK TO THRIVE

Cooking for ourselves is the key to vibrant health. When we shop for ourselves, we can select the highest quality ingredients, which offer the most nutrition.

As we cook, the aromas, sights, and sounds ignite our senses. These sensual cues activate the release of appropriate digestive enzymes. Embrace meal preparation to strengthen your mind-body connection. According to Chinese philosophy, giving full attention to the preparation of a dish auspiciously influences the health and good fortune of the chef and those who eat the meal.

Mealtime Mindfulness

Our frame of mind at mealtime will affect how well we feel physically. When we approach eating in a mindful manner and take the time to sit down in a quiet, comfortable place, the food will be digested well.

You may recall a dinner enjoyed with friends by candlelight at a lovely table setting. You probably remember how delicious the meal was and how good you felt the rest of the evening.

In contrast, on another occasion you may have stood over your sink and in a rush gulped down a sandwich or a piece of pizza left over from the night before, hardly chewing or tasting what you were eating. What kind of memory do you have of that meal? Did you feel satisfied afterward, or did you find it hard to concentrate and perform at your best?

Giving thanks at the beginning of a meal creates a peaceful atmosphere at the table and harmonizes mind, body, and spirit before receiving the food. Mealtime can be one of our finest rituals. Sharing food with good friends and loved ones brings us closer to each other. When we cook we engage all five senses, which is essential for optimal digestion. Enjoy the powerful effect of preparing and sharing your own meals. Bon appétit!

ORGANIZE YOUR KITCHEN

An attractive, functional kitchen makes meal preparation easy and fun.

- The right utensils result in efficiency.
- Place utensils where they are most often used.
- Hang pots and pans near the stove.
- Place a sieve/colander near your sink.
- Keep lids handy by placing a lid rack on the refrigerator or counter near the stove.
- Keep knives sharp and pans shiny.
- Build or install "open" shelves to display beautiful serving bowls and have jars of spices within easy reach.

PLAYING "BEAT THE CLOCK"

There can be unexpected consequences from multitasking and always being in a rush. When I was a designer for a Paris-based lingerie firm on Madison Avenue in that faster-than-the-speed-of-light-city New York, I was on an adrenaline high 24/7 without a drop of caffeine. The world of fashion required one to be out and about so I went out almost every night. I took advantage of every opportunity to socialize that came my way. I was so engaged in life that I was unaware that I rarely slept more than five hours a night.

The inevitable outcome of this nonstop lifestyle struck without warning. Early one morning, I awakened with an excruciating pain in my neck that made it impossible for me to go to work. It turned out to be a serious condition that required a variety of therapies and several weeks of treatment. Because the pressures of the fashion industry intensified the pain, I was forced to leave my job. I fell into depression from the sudden change in my life. One evening, a friend called and invited me to join her on a seven-day trip to Jamaica over the Easter holidays. I was ready for a change, and taking a break from Manhattan sounded great!

On the island, we visited tropical rain forests and white sandy beaches lined with coconut trees. Mysteriously, seemingly out of nowhere, tall Rastafarian men would appear, face me and say, "Slow down. Take your time," and then disappear back into the coconut grove. People we met would ask, "Are you the older sister?" This caused me to suspect that my fast-paced lifestyle was accelerating my aging as I was 5 years younger than my friend.

I returned to New York refreshed and relaxed with a new perspective. A week later, I was sitting upstairs at the Oyster Bar in Grand Central Station waiting to meet a friend. It was rush hour, and commuters were hurrying back and forth to catch their trains. As I watched them, the words of those Jamaican wise men echoed in my mind: "Slow down. Take your time."

"What is the point of rushing?" I thought. The faster one moves, the greater the pressure to perform, to do, and to be. Where does it end? I felt so content observing the hectic commuters

while sipping my Perrier with a slice of lime and reflecting on how slowing down allowed me to enjoy the beauty of the moment.

The perception of clock time varies across cultures and locations. In Mexico, there is always *mañana,* meaning at some time in the future. In Indonesia, the term *rubber time* describes boat and bus departures that are uncertain, while in Germany and Switzerland, being "on time" is considered a virtue.

Even though developing a harmonious relationship with time schedules can be a challenge in modern-day life, mastering the art of timing means shifting eating habits from touch-and-go to well-managed and truly nourishing. Do you often find yourself grabbing a bite on the run or skipping meals completely because of appointments, meetings, or feeling that you cannot stop to eat? Perhaps it's time to become master rather than servant of the clock. With persistent effort, a relaxed state of mind while cooking and having a nourishing meal can be yours.

Think about your lifestyle and your routine today. If you are not in the habit of cooking for yourself, start by taking some steps to rearrange your schedule. Set aside time for preparing and enjoying meals. Begin by cooking for yourself two to three times a week. Make an extra portion so you will have a serving left over for lunch or dinner the next day.

Be adventurous. Shop at farmers markets. Try new recipes. Learn which pots, pans, and utensils are best for preparing simple meals and keep a pantry of basic ingredients on hand. Make cooking fun by inviting friends over to assist you with preparation. Sharing mealtime with a companion can multiply dining pleasure.

As you improve your eating habits and sharpen your cooking skills, you will experience greater vitality and self sufficiency.

Culinary Mastery

By devoting time to meal preparation you will develop cooking skills and expand your culinary repertoire. Become familiar with ingredients and cooking techniques. The formula is simple: consistent practice puts you on the path to chefhood. Skills of mastery are acquired by careful observation. Be alert and attentive, watching for cues from what you see, smell, hear, touch and taste. Responding to sensory feedback as you prepare each dish is more valuable than mastering intricate recipes.

Cooking by instinct is the key to culinary advancement. Start with the freshest seasonal produce, spices, and herbs. No recipe will ever turn out better than what you start with. Touch the ingredients to become familiar with their texture and discover the most suitable method of preparation. Smell and taste the foods and seasonings on their own and in combination with other ingredients to understand how they work together.

Start with a recipe that appeals to you and follow it exactly to see how the ingredients are used and how the dish turns out. Keep a notebook to record what you made, what worked, what went wrong, and how you can adjust the ingredients to improve results. Your notes will be a valuable reference in developing your own cooking style.

Doing kitchen tasks by hand is a great way to learn. Experienced chefs swear there is a noticeable difference in the taste and texture when food is hand chopped, whipped, and mixed. Convenience appliances save time, but relying on them does not advance cooking skills.

The more often you cook, the greater your ability to adapt and adjust will become. An attentive mind during food preparation builds skill to make the simplest dish a work of art. Why not try a recipe from this cookbook and treat yourself to something delicious!

FRIENDS AND FOOD

Meaningful relationships and good food — what can add more pleasure to our lives? Friendships nourish our hearts and souls, and food nourishes our bodies and minds.

When traveling in foreign lands communication can be limited or even nonexistent due to language barriers and cultural differences. What amazes me is that even without conversation, it's possible to make friends by sharing a meal. I have always enjoyed trying new foods that are prepared and served in new ways. Being open and receptive has helped me gain an appreciation for other cultures and ways of life.

While living in Japan, I took an excursion to a countryside village outside Kyoto that was famous for *shibori*, a traditional dyeing technique in which an intricate pattern is created by binding, stretching, folding, twisting, and compressing the fabric.

Entering the artisans' workshop, I was warmly greeted by the family of artisans who had been practicing this textile art for several generations. Their grandmother took charge of entertaining me. We sat down together and were served *macha* tea and traditional sweets.

As we sipped our green tea and nibbled our Japanese sweets, the eighty-year-old woman spoke to me in Japanese, almost none of which I could understand. In response, I nodded and occasionally added, "*Ah so desu-ka?*" (Is that so?). We smiled and laughed as we enjoyed our sweets. She was an absolute delight, and we became friends over tea.

As I prepared to leave, she presented me with a delicate *shibori* handkerchief for which I thanked her by saying "*Ureshii, ureshii*" (happy, happy). I left smiling in a cheerful state of mind.

Whether at home or abroad, sharing a home-cooked meal can enrich relationships and lift spirits. Want more quality time with friends and loved ones? Get together for some kitchen fun!

Eat the Freshest Foods For Utmost Vitality

Whether growing in the ground or on a tree, fruits and vegetables are alive with energy, or *prana*, a Sanskrit word meaning "life force." Once harvested, this energetic quality begins to diminish. During transit from farm to stores and while on display at the supermarket, they continue to lose even more of their vitality. To get the most energetically potent nourishment, seek out the freshest produce. The following suggestions offer ways to bring the freshest harvest to your table.

Plant a Garden

Fruits and vegetables that you grow yourself are energetically potent foods. Whether you have a large yard or simply a balcony or porch, you can cultivate your own garden. All that's needed is sunlight, soil, water, and some containers. Having your own garden space gives you the chance to harvest fresh produce that is ripened naturally. After all, what can compare with the sweet taste of tomatoes picked straight from the vine or carrots taken right from the earth? Because they have remained on the vine or in the ground until fully ripe, they are the most flavorful. Try experimenting with a home garden and enjoy wholesome food with higher levels of energy and maximum nutrition.

Join a Community Garden

Neighborhood gardens are fun places to connect with like-minded people and to broaden your food awareness. Such sites may comprise one large tract of land or consist of several individual plots. These gardens are generally located in designated public places, such as a school yard or an open dirt lot. When you participate in a community garden, you can enjoy fresh air and outdoor activity while developing the self-reliance that comes from doing things yourself, like growing your own food.

To find a garden in your area or to learn how to start one yourself, go to the website of the American Community Garden Association:

www.communitygarden.org

Shop at Farmers Markets

Going to farmers markets gives us a chance to buy fresher, healthier, seasonal foods. Becoming acquainted with local farmers, we can buy organic produce from growers whose sustainable planting approach results in nutrient dense soil and more nutritional food. Unlike business owners in modern large-scale agriculture, local growers choose to offer heirloom varieties of produce known for their superior quality and beneficial phytochemicals, the trace elements necessary for maintaining homeostasis in the body.

Buying directly from family farms protects regional farmland and gives farmers a bigger profit margin so they can spend more on quality soil inputs, fair wages for workers, and better equipment.

Farm-Fresh Produce Deliveries

If you don't have time to shop or are unable to leave home, a weekly home or office produce delivery service is a good solution. These fruits and vegetables are usually harvested just before scheduled delivery in order to maximize freshness. Each box of Community Supported Agriculture (CSA) contains an assortment of seasonal fruits and vegetables. Because local farmers value your business, they may add a little extra produce to show customer appreciation.

Ordering farm baskets supports sustainable agriculture and conscientious business practices.

To find a farm or farmer's market near you go to:

www.localharvest.org

INVISIBLE ELEMENTS IN OUR FOOD

There is more to food than nutritional value. Every bite we take is alive with energy from the earth, the sun, the rain, and the people who grew and harvested it. The quality of energy in what we eat can affect how alive we feel and how productive we are throughout the day.

You may have heard of the Chinese term *chi* referring to vital force or energy that flows through all living beings. *Sheng chi* is light, bright energy; and *sha chi* is dark, dull energy. Foods grown in harmony with nature and with respect for the environment are full of *sheng chi*, or positive energy. Foods that are subjected to pesticides, harmful chemicals, genetic modification, or radiation are filled with *sha chi*, or negative energy. To experience greater vitality and save our land from unnecessary harmful chemicals, choose foods grown in the most wholesome, sustainable way.

In preparation, the cook's state of mind will influence how well those who eat it will feel during the meal as well as after eating. For instance, a chef who is angry or unhappy can cause the positive *sheng chi* qualities to take on negative *sha chi* characteristics.

A fanciful example that illustrates this is seen in the Mexican film, "Water for Chocolate." In the story, a young girl, Tita, and the son of a neighbor are in love, but her mother forbids her daughter to marry. To always be close to his love the young man follows his father's advice and marries her older sister.

For her sister's wedding, Tita must help with preparation. While making the dessert, the young girl is overcome by sadness and begins to cry. Her tears of sorrow fall like rain into the kettle of chocolate that she is stirring; and when the guests at the wedding eat the dessert, tears fill their eyes and soon everyone is sobbing.

Preparing food when we are upset or feeling down is not advised, as it can have a negative effect on those who eat it. When we prepare meals lovingly and in a joyful state of mind the food will be digested well and we will feel truly satisfied.

Fortify Your Body with Essential Fatty Acids

Essential fatty acids (EFAs) serve to provide energy and move oxygen through the blood to hydrate our cells, skin, and other organs. EFAs must be obtained through our diet daily because our body cannot produce them by itself. Omega-3 (alpha-linoleic acid) and omega-6 (linoleic acid) are known to be essential for humans.

Observational studies have demonstrated that these fatty acids consumed in the proper ratio can reduce inflammation and lower the risk of heart disease. Most people get sufficient amounts of omega-6 but are often deficient in omega-3. Dr. Akil Palanisamy, MD, author of *The Paleovedic Diet,* recommends aiming for a ratio of either 4:1 or 5:1 omega-3 to omega-6.

Plant sources of omega-3 include Brussel sprouts, walnuts, and chia, hemp, and flax seeds. To maximize the absorption of the essential fatty acids in these seeds, buy them whole and grind them in small amounts in a coffee grinder or blender before adding them to foods. Store ground seeds in a tightly closed glass jar in the refrigerator. Once or twice a day, sprinkle a teaspoon or two on cereals, salads, cooked vegetables, grains, or legumes.

If you take omega-3 supplements in gelatin capsules made from fish or plant based oil, check for possible rancidity by piercing one of the capsules from the bottle. If the oil has a foul smell or tastes even a little off, return it to the store.

EFAs in nuts and seeds can be destroyed by heat, light, and oxygen, so store seeds and nuts in the refrigerator to protect the fragile oils they contain.

Beneficial Oils & Fats

AVOCADO OIL
This omega-3 rich oil makes a good base for salad dressings (page 203). It is fairly stable when heated for sautéing spices.

BUTTER
Organic butter from grass-fed cows can be used to give foods a richer flavor. It is good for sautéing at moderate temperatures and for spreading on bread and baked items. You may want to try cultured organic butter, which melts deliciously on the tongue and is especially good for baking.

FLAXSEED OIL
The highest plant source of omega-3, this oil may be taken in a capsule as a supplement or in liquid form, though some find the flavor of flaxseed oil too strong. In that case, try sprinkling freshly ground flax seeds on food. Ground flax seeds have a nutty flavor and are just as nutritious as the oil. Flaxseed oil is fragile and should not be exposed to heat or used for cooking. Store in the refrigerator and take note of its expiration date.

EXTRA-VIRGIN OLIVE OIL
Best drizzled over salads and cooked vegetables, this oil may be used for light sautéing of spices, herbs, and vegetables over medium-low heat. See interview on pages 34-37.

GHEE
This ultra-clarified butter is good for cooking and sautéing spices. It is lactose-free and safe for those who are lactose intolerant. It has a nutty flavor. See pages 56-57 for more information and recipe.

HEMP SEED OIL
A rich source of essential fatty acids, hemp seed oil has a subtle, nutty flavor. Drizzle a teaspoon over soups, salads, grains, and cooked veggies to raise omega-3 intake. Store in the refrigerator and be sure to use it before the expiration date.

PUMPKIN SEED OIL
Tasting like pumpkin seeds, this oil has a deep amber color. Add to casseroles and stuffings for a unique flavor. The toasted variety offers an additional flavor possibility.

SESAME OIL

This oil stands up well to heat and is good for stir-frying. Toasted sesame oil, which is often used in Asian cooking, can add a distinct flavor to sauces, dressings, and marinades.

WALNUT OIL

Use walnut oil in salad dressings or drizzle over cooked vegetables. This delicate oil should not be heated. Buy organic, cold-pressed walnut oil in small quantities and taste before each use to check for rancidity.

Purchasing, Cooking, and Storage Tips

- Buy oils that are labeled "cold-pressed" (extracted and processed without heat) whenever possible.
- Store oils in a cool, dark place to keep them safe from oxygenation. Keep nuts, seeds, and grains in the refrigerator.
- Buy oils in quantities that will be consumed within two to three months, and be aware of their limited shelf life.
- If oils, grains, seeds, nuts, nut butters, crackers, cookies, or chips smell or taste "off," this indicates that the oils they contain are rancid and they should be discarded.
- To prevent a bitter taste and the formation of toxic compounds, do not allow fats or oils to reach the smoking point in cooking.

INTERVIEW

Olive Oil, A Sacred Blessing
Dan Sciabica, Nick Sciabica & Sons

The cultivation of olive trees is one of the oldest activities of civilization, even preceding written language. There are over 140 references to olive oil in the Bible, and olive trees have been a symbol of peace and good will for thousands of years.

Today pouring a few drops of olive oil over salads and vegetables adds the blessing of good health. Studies have shown that olive oil helps control cholesterol, lower the risk of colon cancer, and improve digestion. The way olive oil is processed affects the health-giving properties it contains.

To learn more about olive oil production, I contacted Nick Sciabica & Sons in Modesto, California. This family has been producing olive oil since 1936, longer than any other producer in the United States. Speaking with Dan Sciabica, the grandson of the company's founder, Nicola (Nick) Sciabica, I was impressed by his vast experience and knowledge.

How did your family get started in olive oil production, Dan?

When my Grandfather Nicola saw the beautiful olive trees in California that had been planted by Spanish missionaries, he wanted to start an olive oil production business. My father, Joseph, agreed, and they started the business together in 1936. My grandfather had worked in olive oil production in Sicily at the turn of the last century. He carried traditional knowledge, and my father, who was full of enthusiasm for the project, developed the business side.

I read in your brochure that your family business represents four generations. How have you managed to be successful for so many years?

We love what we do, and we work together as a family. We follow my grandfather's and my father's tradition of honoring the expertise of our elders, while at the same time welcoming the younger generation's new ideas. My father always listened to us when we wanted to try something new. Now my brother's son, Jonathan, and my daughter, Christa, are adding their inventiveness to our family tradition.

Producing an olive oil of the highest quality must require careful attention. What are some of your family's secrets?

We take special care in the selection of the olives. Only the finest olives can produce the highest-quality olive oil. Maintaining its purity is our goal, as the closer the olive oil is to its natural state, the higher the quality will be.

Is making olive oil a complicated process?

It's basically two steps: First, the olives are ground and crushed with a stainless-steel hammer mill. Next, a malaxer, a machine that kneads the pulp like bread dough, is used to open the cells in the flesh of the olives and release the oil. According to my grandfather, both steps were done with a stone mill in Sicily.

You said one of the secrets of producing exceptional olive oil is in the selection of the olives. Do you pick the olives by hand?

Yes. We climb a ladder and use a bucket with a strap over one shoulder.

That seems like a lot of work. Are there other ways of harvesting olives?

Some producers put a tarp under the tree and hit the branches with a long pole. There are also mechanized harvesters, but there is something special about touching the olives with your hands. You feel that you and the fruit are one.

What are some of the vital factors in producing a quality olive oil?

Getting the oil away from the olives as soon as possible is crucial, as the water they contain can cause them to ferment, and we can't get a quality product from fermented fruit. Transporting the olives to the mill before they start to ferment is a top priority.

You said the end product is the culmination of a year's work. Could you explain?

The oil can be taken from the olives in less than an hour, but the olive trees need attention year-round. After the last harvest in March, the trees are pruned. Pruning yearly and severely is important to ensure an abundant crop.

The trees must be well irrigated in April in preparation for their blossoming in May. Trees are constantly monitored to protect them from disease and from the olive fruit fly. A stable, peaceful environment is necessary for the olive trees to flourish. It is a real labor of love.

Are certain months of the year more critical than others?

April and May. What happens in this period, from the appearance of blossoms until the fruit begins to grow, determines the quality and quantity of the harvest.

In spring, our trees may have lots of blossoms, but if weather conditions are harsh, the blossoms drop and the trees bear little fruit. Sometimes hot winds in May and June can burn the olives right off the trees. Production is dependent on the forces of nature. Once June passes, the olives are relatively safe until they are harvested.

How do you know when the olives are ready to be picked?

The strength of the stem indicates when the fruit is ready, and that varies according to the variety. We must watch our trees continuously to determine the proper time. As soon as the stems no longer hold the olives on the trees, we harvest them immediately. We cannot use fruit that has fallen to the ground.

We hear a lot about "cold-pressed" olive oil today. What is that exactly?

It means the oil is extracted without heat. "Cold pressing" guarantees more flavor and nutritional value. Heat in production causes olive oil to deteriorate. Olive oils from the first pressing contain the most nutritional value.

Is there much difference in taste between refined and cold-pressed olive oils?

There is no comparison. Highly-refined olive oils are tasteless, while the taste of unfiltered, extra-virgin olive oil is phenomenal.

Is there much variation in the character and taste of olive oils?

Their character and taste are determined by many factors. Some oils are intense, some are delicate, some taste flowery, and some nutty. Green olives from the fall season have a flavor that is intense and tart, while olives harvested from November through February produce a sweeter olive oil. In early spring, the olive oil has a delicate flavor that is reminiscent of butter.

What makes olive oil so beneficial, Dan?

The polyphenols. Polyphenols are antioxidants that have the ability to neutralize harmful free radicals that cause cellular damage. To gauge the level of polyphenols, try a small spoon of the oil on its own. A tartness in taste and a tingling sensation in the back of the throat when the olive oil is swallowed indicates a high level of polyphenols. The stronger the tartness, the more potent are the polyphenols.

When we see "extra virgin" on the label, what does that mean?

That means the olive oil comes from the first cold pressing and is the highest grade. The free fatty acid contents must be no more than 0.8% in order to qualify as extra virgin.

What is the best way to protect olive oil from deterioration?

Store in a cool, dark place away from the stove. Long-necked bottles protect oil from exposure to air, but as the olive oil is consumed, there is less and less oil in the bottle and more and more air. Therefore, it is best to buy a quantity that will be used within two to three months.

I thanked Dan and wished him and his family well. Understanding the labor that goes into our food increases our appreciation for the nourishment it provides.

Liberate Yourself From Sugar

Cutting down on your consumption of sweets is one of the best steps you can take toward optimal health.

In this chapter, you'll find ways to decrease sugar intake and lower the risk of obesity, diabetes, and other degenerative diseases. *Lick the Sugar Habit* by Nancy Appleton explains how seriously sugar can disturb our body chemistry.

Research has shown that sugar is addictive because having only a little creates a desire for more. Eliminating sugar from our diet can cause withdrawal symptoms such as headaches, mood swings, fatigue, and depression. Cutting sugar consumption can be a serious challenge because it is found in almost every packaged food that we buy. Awareness, effort, determination, and perseverance are required to get free from its grasp.

Several of Nancy Appleton's suggestions on ways to eliminate sweets follow.

Know Where Sugar May Be Hidden

Sugar is a common ingredient in breads, seasonings, bagels, muffins, crackers, dressings, soups, sauces and gravies, packaged meals, frozen dinners, and chips (see list page 44).

Glucose, fructose, and sucrose are the main forms of sugar. Glucose is a simple sugar, and the end product that is produced in the body when carbohydrates are digested. Fructose is the form of sugar present in fruit. Fructose is also present in a food additive known as HFCS, high-fructose corn syrup. Sucrose is formed by one molecule of glucose linked to one molecule of fructose. White sugar is sucrose that is derived from sugarcane or sugar beets.

Dextrin is a carbohydrate that is formed by the hydrolysis of starches and is used as a thickening agent in dietary supplements. Dextrose is a simple sugar that is chemically identical to glucose and is made from corn that is often genetically modified (GMO). It is commonly used in processed foods and as a sweetener in baked products.

Read Labels Carefully

High-fructose corn syrup (HFCS), corn sweetener, dextrose, maltodextrin, sucrose, and glucose are the most harmful forms of sugar (page 45). When they appear at the beginning of the ingredient list, this indicates that the product contains a large quantity.

Sugar may be labeled raw, organic, unprocessed, pure, or natural. Such descriptive words may mislead consumers into believing that such forms of sugar are not harmful. All forms of sugar contain the same number of calories, are chemically classified as sucrose, and affect body chemistry in the same way. In other words, the less of any sweetener you consume, whether processed or natural, the better off you will be.

Phase Sugar Out

Mark a date on your calendar when you intend to stop sugar consumption, and then decrease your intake accordingly. Learn how to use stevia in place of sugar (pages 42-43).

Stay focused on your long term goal and congratulate yourself when you achieve it!

Keep a Sugar-Free Home

Throw out all forms of sugar, including sugar-laden beverages. Do not keep cookies, candies, baked goods, ice cream, or sodas to offer guests. Eliminating such products can strengthen your resolve and minimize cravings and temptations.

Give Up Soft Drinks

Replace soft drinks with distilled, spring, or filtered water. Try adding a slice of fresh lemon or lime for flavor and extra vitamin C. Drinking herbal teas can serve to nourish, cleanse and heal the body as well as aid digestion. See Healing Beverages (pages 95-105).

Set Limits

Limit yourself to 1/2 to 1 teaspoon a day of any natural sweetener such as raw honey, maple syrup, barley malt, or coconut sugar.

The latest U.S. dietary guidelines recommend that sugar compose no more than 10 percent of the total calories consumed in a day. A person who eats 2,000 calories a day could have as much as 1/4 cup (2 oz/60 g) of sugar under these guidelines. I recommend that white sugar be eliminated altogether and that natural sweeteners be kept to a minimum.

Delay

When you crave a sugary food, resist the impulse to snack for at least twenty minutes. Distract yourself by doing something you enjoy or taking care of something on your "to do" list. Cravings usually disappear after a few minutes. The less frequently we give into our temptations, the stronger our resistance becomes.

Tackle Temptation

Avoid situations where you will encounter sweets. Instead of meeting a friend at the local bakery or cafe, go for a nature walk or prepare a healthy meal together. Stay away from the cookie, cake, and candy section at the market. Pack a piece of fruit or a homemade treat when going out, so you don't just grab a sugary snack when hunger strikes. See recipes for Snacks and Appetizers (page 119-130).

Understanding Connections and Self Awareness

If you reach for a soft drink or a piece of candy, pause and ask yourself why. Are you feeling anxious, bored, fatigued, or depressed? Are you looking for comfort or something to do? Awareness is power. Understanding our psyche and reasons for our cravings can strengthen our will power.

Try Sweet Vegetables and Spices

To satisfy cravings for something sweet, try carrots, beets, sweet potatoes, or winter squash. These vegetables have natural sugars, contain fiber, and can be satisfying nutritious alternatives. Cinnamon, nutmeg, cloves, and cardamom are sweet spices that have health-giving properties while they enhance flavor. See Medicinal Spices, pages 61-68.

Eat Protein in Small Portions

Protein breaks down into amino acids when absorbed, resulting in the release of glycogen (stored sugar) which raises the blood glucose level. In time as the blood glucose level drops, you may find yourself craving a sugary snack. Pay attention to how you feel after eating protein foods. If you notice that you feel like having a sweet, try reducing protein portions at mealtimes. Some protein foods may create stronger cravings than others. Nancy Appleton's recommendation is that all protein foods be eaten in small portions.

A Word About Corn

A common source of sugar in processed food is high fructose corn syrup (HFCS). If you have been eating lots of packaged and processed foods be aware that corn and corn by-products may be triggering your sugar cravings. If this is happening, eliminate corn from your diet for three months to decrease your cravings for sweets.

Exercise, Exercise, Exercise

Physical activity releases toxins, burns calories, and builds muscle strength. Regular exercise benefits our health and keeps us active and away from the cookie jar.

Be Patient and Persistent

Changing any habit takes time. If you do not succeed on the first attempt, note what went wrong and keep trying. It takes repetition to establish the desirable habits we are striving for. The less sugar you consume, the less you will want.

Get Support

Buddy up with a friend to strengthen your commitment. If you have been a sugar addict for many years, check with your doctor. Regular sessions with a nutritionist or health coach can be encouraging and helpful for establishing healthy eating habits especially in moments of doubt, frustration, or temptation.

Natural Sweeteners

Natural sweeteners such as maple syrup, raw honey, molasses, and coconut sugar may seem like healthier alternatives to white sugar, but they affect the body in the same undesirable way. For this reason, it's prudent to keep daily consumption of any sweetener to no more than a teaspoon. While natural sweeteners contain some essential vitamins and minerals, they would have to be consumed in such large quantities that the caloric count would likely outweigh any substantial nutritional benefits.

Stevia is a natural sweetener that is an exception as it has zero calories, and research indicates that there is no significant pancreatic response. One drop of liquid stevia in a cup of tea sweetens the beverage just as a teaspoon of sugar or other natural sweetener would do.

SUBSTITUTING STEVIA FOR SUGAR

Derived from the dried and ground leaves of *Stevia rebaudiana*, stevia is sold as a dietary supplement in various forms. The leaves from this plant have been consumed for centuries by the indigenous peoples in South America.

Because stevia is 100 to 300 times sweeter than table sugar, a minimal amount is all that is needed. Using too much can impart an unpleasant aftertaste. Combining stevia with a natural sweetener such as maple syrup can improve resulting flavor. For example, when a recipe calls for 1/2 cup (4 fl oz/120 ml) maple syrup, you can use 1/4 cup (2 fl oz/60 ml) maple syrup, 1/4 cup (2 fl oz/60ml) filtered water, and 5 to 6 drops of liquid stevia. Replace 1 tablespoon maple syrup with 1 teaspoon maple syrup, 2 teaspoons water, and 3 to 4 drops liquid stevia.

Baking With Stevia

Baking with stevia requires some ingredient adjustments. It is recommended that no more than half of the sugar measurement in a recipe be replaced by stevia due to the moisture, browning, and rising effects of sugar. For baking purposes, seek out granulated stevia that is specifically intended as substitute for sugar. Recipes calling for 1/4 cup (1 3/4 oz/50 g) of sugar or less are ideal for stevia substitution.

A vital quality that sugar provides in baked goods is bulk. In recipes that call for sugar, stevia can be substituted as long as it is combined with foods that provide supplemental moisture and bulk. For example, instead of 1 cup of sugar, use 1/3 cup (80 ml/90g) of a mashed banana plus 1 1/2 teaspoons liquid stevia. Common bulking agents include yogurt, egg whites, pumpkin, pureed fruit, and unsweetened applesauce. If the recipe already has a bulk agent in it, then reduce the 1/3 cup (80 ml/90g) of the bulk agent to 1/4 cup (2 fl oz/60 ml).

Forms of Stevia

<u>Extract</u>: The liquid dropper bottle works well in sweetening beverages, sauces, puddings, preserves, and pie fillings. This is the most potent form of stevia, as 1/2 teaspoon stevia adds as much sweetness as 1/4 cup (1 3/4 oz/50 g) sugar. Liquid stevia that does not contain alcohol has less of an aftertaste. This is the form I use and prefer.

<u>White Powder</u>: Powdered stevia is similar to confectioners' sugar but can have a bitter aftertaste. To avoid the aftertaste, use this form sparingly or combine with a little coconut palm sugar or xylitol. It is not recommended for baking because it is too difficult to achieve the same sweetness as sugar without imparting a bitter aftertaste.

<u>Granulated</u>: Specifically formulated for replacing sugar in baked goods, granulated stevia can ensure good results. Refer to package directions for exact measurements to use in substituting stevia for sugar. To take the mystery out of substituting stevia for sugar, one specific name brand now on the market for baking is Pyure Organic Stevia All Purpose Blend Sweetener. It is available in natural food stores and on line.

Other Alternatives
- Instead of granulated sugar, an equivalent amount of xylitol may be substituted.
- Instead of brown sugar, try coconut palm sugar, a minimally processed natural sweetener.

<u>Note</u>: Stevia does not caramelize and cannot be used in desserts that involve caramelizing, such as crème brulée.

Conversions

1 teaspoon sugar = 1 to 2 drops liquid stevia or 1/16 teaspoon white or green stevia powder

1 tablespoon sugar = 4 to 6 drops liquid stevia or 1/4 teaspoon white or green stevia powder

1 cup (8 oz/250 g) sugar = 1 teaspoon liquid stevia or 2 teaspoons white or green stevia powder

Products Where Sugar Is Found

Sugar is frequently an ingredient in products where you might least expect it. White refined sugar and high-fructose corn syrup (HFCS) are inexpensive to use commercially, so they are often present in large quantities in processed foods and drinks. To be sure you are not buying products with unhealthful sweeteners, always check ingredient labels carefully. The following products commonly contain white refined sugar, high-fructose corn syrup (HFCS), and artificial sweeteners:

- Applesauce
- Baby formula
- Bacon
- Bagels
- Bread mixes
- Breads
- Breakfast bars
- Breakfast cereals
- Canned fruits
- Canned meats
- Canned soups
- Canned vegetables
- Chewing gum
- Cocktail mixers
- Cough syrup
- Craisins
- Dried fruit
- Fruit juices
- Jamba Juice drinks
- Ketchup
- Luna bars
- Lunch meat
- Mustard
- Pancake mixes
- Peanut butter
- Probiotics, chewable
- Protein powder
- Red wine
- Relish
- Rolls
- Salad dressings
- Snapple tea
- Soup mixes
- Starbuck's Yogurt Parfait
- Subway Sweet Teriyaki Chicken sandwich
- Tomato sauce
- Vitamin water
- Waffle mix
- Yoplait

Sweeteners to Avoid

White sugar is highly processed and often bleached. Both HFCS and white sugar lack nutritional value and are rapidly metabolized. When consumed, an initial feeling of enhanced energy may be experienced. Then an hour or so later, a sudden drop in energy can occur along with unwanted side effects that disrupt concentration and productivity.

High-fructose corn syrup (HFCS) is frequently found in soft drinks, baked goods, and processed foods. Often genetically modified, this sweetener is made by extracting fructose from corn. Then it is combined in a concentrated form with glucose.

The fructose in HFCS is processed in the liver and produces a form of fat known as a triglyceride. Research has linked a number of degenerative diseases to the consumption of HFCS, which is a well-founded reason to phase out soft drinks and processed foods from your diet.

Common Artificial Sweeteners

- Acesulfame K (acesulfame potassium, Ace K, or ACK)
- Aspartame (NutraSweet, Equal)
- Neotame (Newtame)
- Saccharin (Sweet'N Low)
- Sucralose (Splenda)

(See Appendix page 238 for a list of products with artifical sweeteners.)

Words such as *diet, zero calories, reduced sugar, reduced calories, low calorie,* or *sugar-free* are commonplace on the labels of foods and beverages containing artificial sweeteners. Read ingredient lists carefully to avoid consumption of these unnatural sweeteners.

These additives are intensely sweet and are as far from natural as you can get. While many are recognized as safe by the United States Food and Drug Administration (FDA), there is concern that artificial sweeteners may reduce healthful bacteria in the intestines, and thus compromise the immune system. Some research indicates that these unnatural sugar substitutes may produce cravings for high-calorie foods and diminish the desire for fresh fruits and vegetables.

Replace Anti-Nutrient Foods with Nutrient-Rich Alternatives

Low-nutrient foods, also known as "empty calories," have little to no nutritional value. Refined sugar, white flour, soft drinks, and highly-processed oils fall under the low-nutrient classification. For your good health choose nutrient-rich alternatives as shown in this chart.

Anti-Nutrient Foods	Nutrient-Rich Foods
Refined white flour	Whole-grain flours, gluten-free flours
Refined white sugar	Natural sweeteners, Stevia (pages 42-43)
Margarine	Butter, ghee, olive oil, nut butters
Highly-processed oils and fats	Ghee, olive oil
Packaged cereals	Homemade cereals (pages 112-113)
Crackers, chips	Organic nuts and seeds
Candy, cookies, cakes, pies	Fresh and dried fruits, especially dates
Packaged, processed foods	Home cooked meals with fresh ingredients
Soft drinks	Filtered water with lemon or lime, herbal tea

Gluten-Free Whole Grains

Whole grains are an excellent source of complex carbohydrates, fiber, vitamins, minerals and proteins. Their high-fiber content cleanses the digestive system and keeps it functioning optimally. Furthermore, their complex molecular structure makes them slow to break down, resulting in sustained energy for several hours.

These whole grains are naturally gluten-free. However, if processed in a facility where grains containing gluten are present, the end product may also contain gluten. So for those who are gluten-intolerant, be sure to check the label for the words "gluten-free."

AMARANTH

The tiny round seeds of this ancient Aztec food resemble its close relative quinoa. A complete protein, amaranth is rich in calcium and magnesium. It also contains iron, folate, and the amino acid lysine. It is said to be beneficial for the lungs. The seeds can be ground into flour in a blender for use in baking. Amaranth can serve as a substitute for polenta, a thickener for soups, or simply enjoyed as a breakfast cereal (page 109).

BROWN RICE

High in B vitamins, brown rice contains three times the fiber of white rice. This rice comes in short, medium, and long-grained varieties. Short and medium grains are thicker, chewier in texture, and take longer to cook than long-grain rice. Short-grain rice has a warming effect and is good to eat in autumn and winter. Alternatively long-grain rice has a cooling effect and is best served in spring and summer according to Ayurveda. Before cooking, soak rice for 30 to 40 minutes in water and rinse to remove arsenic.

BUCKWHEAT

An alkaline-forming grain, buckwheat comes in three forms: unhulled groats, hulled groats, and flour. High in minerals and vitamin E, this grain is considered a blood builder. Because it stimulates circulation in the hands and feet when eaten regularly, buckwheat can offer relief to sufferers of varicose veins.

MILLET

A buff-yellow grain, millet has a fluffy texture once cooked. As an excellent source of B vitamins, vitamin E, iron, magnesium and potassium, millet can boost energy, balance over-acidic conditions, and benefit the digestive system. It is the best grain to eat on a weight-loss diet. Spring is a good time to serve millet. It can be ground into flour for baking and dry toasting millet before cooking can heighten its flavor. A combination of millet with quinoa or white basmati rice makes a novel alternative to the standard pilaf (pages 158-159).

OATS

A rich source of B complex vitamins, oats are highly beneficial to the nervous system. In addition to lowering cholesterol oats contain good fats that can assist in weight loss. Oats are said to relieve insomnia, strengthen bones and cardiac muscles, normalize thyroid function, and help remedy constipation and indigestion. Oats come in many forms and they are relatively the same nutritionally. (See page 228)

QUINOA

This grain has a mild nutty taste and is a distant relative of other leaf vegetables such as beet, spinach, and chard . Quinoa contains all the essential amino acids, making it a complete protein. It has a low fat content and is easily digested. It can be added to salads and soups and served as a side dish or as a hot cereal for breakfast.

Protecting Grains from Spoilage

- Store whole grains in a cool, dark, and dry place or in the refrigerator to extend their shelf life.
- Glass jars with airtight lids are ideal to protect grains from exposure to air and moisture.
- The natural oils in whole grains can become rancid when exposed to light, heat, and air.
- If they have been in your pantry for more than four months, smell and taste them before using to make sure the oils they contain have not gone rancid. If they smell or taste stale, discard them.

INTERVIEW

From Conventional Farming to Certified Organic:

Tom Dieckmann, Feather River Farms

Feather River Farms, a family farm in Yuba City, California, was established in 1988. In 2009, it became a certified organic farm. Peaches, nectarines, cherries, apricots, and pluots are their specialty. They also have walnut trees and grow melons, broccoli, cabbage, and winter squash. They sell around 100,000 pounds of produce a year and have been selling at local farmers' markets for 25 years.

I first met Tom Dieckmann, the owner of Feather River Farms, in 2012 at the Saturday Grand Lake farmers' market in Oakland, California. His stand caught my attention when I saw his display of raw walnuts. Then I noticed a kind of winter squash that I had not seen since I lived in France. Curious, I asked him about it.

During our conversation, I learned that Feather River Farms had been a conventional farm until 2006. That is when Tom and his family decided to convert to organic standards. I wondered what had influenced Tom's decision to farm organically and how he had managed the transition successfully, so I scheduled the following interview:

How did you become interested in farming, Tom?

I was forty years old. I wanted to make a change and was looking for a better way of life. I did not have any background or training in farming but knew I could make it work.

That sounds courageous. Was it difficult to get started?

We started with nothing and leased land and equipment. We worked long hours. It took fifteen years of hard work to see a profit.

You must have learned a lot from this experience. How do you manage to keep your farm profitable?

We grow a variety of fruits and vegetables to keep our production consistent throughout the year. Diversifying extends our growing season and gives us crops to harvest from May through March. I'm constantly experimenting and looking for new crops. Having items that other farmers aren't growing attracts new customers to our stand. One year my mother brought some winter squash seeds back from France. We planted them and they did well, so the following year we planted more and started selling them at farmers markets.

Fruit trees are more of a commitment. After the trees are planted, it takes three years before they bear fruit. We start with thirty trees, or about a third of an acre. If they do well, we plant a whole acre. If not, we pull them out and try another kind of fruit tree. They live for about twenty years.

The walnuts I bought from you were exceptional. Do walnut trees need special care?

They used to be known as a "retirement crop" because when a farmer was close to retirement age he would plant walnut trees. This provided income for the farmer and his family with minimal labor.

Walnut trees do well in California and are one of the easiest crops to grow. It takes 7 years to see a decent crop, but walnut trees live for 60 to 70 years. We've had our trees 10 years.

The oil in walnuts is quite fragile and can easily go rancid. How do you keep the walnuts safe from deterioration?

We remove the walnuts from their shells by hand and keep them in cold storage, sealed in zip-top bags between markets. We take every precaution to protect our nuts from heat, light, and air, the elements responsible for the deterioration.

What motivated you to become an organic farm after doing conventional farming for over fifteen years?

I got tired of the side effects I experienced by using commercial pesticides. Even though I used a mask and was well protected, my lips would burn and I would feel bad for several days after spraying. At first I ignored this, but as the years passed, I could no longer tolerate it.

At the same time, our customers were asking for organic produce. For us, making the transition was a sensible decision based on the desire for better health and to please our customers.

How did you accomplish the conversion?

Making the transition without losing any production was our first concern. I was lucky that the vendor I bought commercial pesticides from also carried organic alternatives. He had been managing orchards on two successful organic farms in the area, so I asked him if he could do the same for Feather River Farms. His experience and knowledge made the transition easier.

I think an increasing number of farmers would change to organic farming if they were given more information about how to manage it successfully. I've talked to some of my neighbors about it, but they are reluctant. This kind of change is frightening for a family farmer because if their crop fails, they could lose their farm.

According to the Organic Trade Association, the organic food industry is "the most heavily-regulated and closely-monitored production system in the United States." Is this true?

Yes. The state establishes regulations and the local agricultural commission carries out inspections to verify compliance. Our farm had to pass a three-year transition period. In 2006, we stopped using chemical pesticides, fertilizers, and weed killers, attaining certification in 2009.

They check our soil to make sure it is free from chemicals; and they examine our books and all the receipts from every product we buy to use on our crops, as well as records of the dates when we sprayed. In order to keep our farm certified we must follow all of these regulations.

I often see products labeled "natural" or "all-natural ingredients." Is this also a certified category?

No. "Natural" foods are not regulated, and they do not need to meet the "certified organic" criteria.

Many consumers wonder why the cost of organic produce is higher than other produce. Can you explain this?

Organic farms do not receive federal subsidies like many conventional farms do. The price of organic produce reflects the true cost of growing it. Chemical-free products are more expensive than commercial brands. The organic fertilizer we use is three times more expensive than chemical fertilizers, and the cost of the products we buy to protect our fruit trees from the oriental fruit moth and peach twig borer is considerably higher than commercial pesticides.

In addition, organic farming is more labor- and management-intensive because without the use of chemicals, we must do more by hand. Certified organic farms are not allowed to use commercial weed killers, so we must hoe and remove weeds manually, which adds to the cost of labor.

The first few years without using commercial weed killers required a lot of extra work. Now there are fewer and fewer weeds because by removing them when they start to grow their seeds do not fall to the ground and sprout again.

That sounds like a real benefit for your farm. What other benefits have you noticed from having an organic farm?

My health is great! I haven't had a cold in years. I'm sixty-three years old and still going strong. Everyone in my family is in good health, and they enjoy participating in the farm. Working on the land keeps us strong, and most of all we enjoy the flavor of our fresh organic produce.

Having an organic farm has also brought us closer to our customers, who love chemical-free produce. And we have become more involved with our community. Last spring, one hundred third-graders visited our farm for an educational field trip. We showed them how to plant broccoli and let them each pick a peach. When the broccoli was harvested, we took eight cases to their school to give the students to take home. The children were delighted that the broccoli they planted grew so well. Now, the school wants to award Feather River Farms a plaque for being a "Community Partner," and this is very special.

HAVE FUN WITH HERBS & SPICES

From the fresh organic herbs at farmers markets to the exotic spices in ethnic food shops, a range of seasoning possibilities is everywhere! Enjoy experimenting with various spices. Keep notes on methods and measurements to repeat successes and fine tune ingredient combinations. Use spices and herbs generously to give dishes a depth of flavor and increase your intake of phytochemicals and antioxidants. Purchase dried herbs and ground spices in quantities you will use within 6 months, as their potency diminishes over time.

French Mediterranean Herbs 54
Herb Combinations 55
Ayurvedic Herbs & Spices 56
Ghee 56
Traditional Japanese Seasoning 59

French Mediterranean Herbs

The commonly used herbs in French cuisine are rich in antioxidants, vitamins, and minerals. These herbs offer a treasure trove of culinary inspiration. They can create subtle dimensions of flavor to intensify or lessen the taste of given ingredients. Both fresh or dried types can be used.

Sweet Herbs
- Aniseeds
- Basil
- Bay Leaves
- Celery
- Chervil
- Cilantro
- Garlic
- Marjoram
- Onions
- Parsley

Peppery Herbs
- Watercress

Bitter/Pungent Herbs
- Oregano
- Rosemary
- Sage
- Thyme

Strongly-Fragrant Herbs
- Fennel
- Lemon verbena
- Peppermint
- Spearmint
- Tarragon

Herb Combinations

Bouquet garni

Bouquet garni refers to a combination of 3 to 6 herbs used to add flavor to sauces, soups, and broths. Fresh herbs are tied together using kitchen twine. Dried herbs are placed in cheese cloth and tied together. The herb combinations are immersed in the pot during cooking and removed before the dish is served. One popular fresh herb combination is parsley, rosemary, thyme, and a bay leaf. A typical dried herb combination consists of thyme, peppercorns, and a bay leaf.

Fines herbes

The classic French combination of *fines herbes* is made up of finely chopped fresh parsley, chives, tarragon, and chervil.

Herbes de Provence

This mixture of dried herbs from the Provence region of France is used to flavor grilled dishes, soups, and stews. This mixture is easy to make and you can create your own signature blend tailored to your tastes. I like this combination from Martha Stewart:

- 3 tablespoons dried thyme
- 2 tablespoons dried savory
- 1 tablespoon dried oregano
- 1 tablespoon dried rosemary
- 2 teaspoons dried marjoram
- 1 tablespoon dried lavender flowers (optional)

Ayurvedic Herbs & Spices

In the holistic Ayurvedic system, spices are considered medicinal and are used to aid digestion, relieve symptoms of illness, and harmonize mind, body, and spirit. Ayurveda classifies all foods including seasonings as sweet, sour, salty, bitter, pungent, or astringent and recommends that each meal contain a combination of these tastes for optimal digestion (See Ayurveda, page 10).

- Asafoetida, or hing
- Cardamom
- Cayenne
- Cilantro
- Cinnamon
- Cloves
- Coriander
- Cumin
- Curry leaves
- Fennel
- Ginger
- Indian green chiles
- Mint
- Nutmeg
- Saffron
- Turmeric

Ghee

Ghee is an ultra-clarified butter from which the water and milk solids have been removed, making it lactose-free. It has a nutty taste and is easy to make at home. In the holistic Ayurvedic system of healing, ghee is combined with medicinal herbs to enhance their healing properties. Because of its richness, ghee can be used more sparingly than butter.

Making Ghee

Sterilize a stainless-steel spoon, fine-mesh sieve, pint glass jar, and lid by immersing them in boiling water or by pouring boiling water over them. Drain, allow to cool, and dry with a clean tea towel. Set aside.

In a medium saucepan, melt 1 pound (500 g) unsalted butter over medium heat.

Stage 1: A milky foam will appear. Turn heat to low and continue to simmer, stirring occasionally.

Stage 2: Clear bubbles appear and the liquid turns golden and begins to crackle.

Stage 3: When the crackling stops and the clear bubbles begin to disappear, this indicates that the ghee is almost ready so watch it closely.

Stage 4: A frothy foam will appear. This means the ghee is done. Remove from heat and let cool for 20 minutes.

After 20 minutes pour through the sterilized fine-mesh sieve into the sterilized glass jar and cover.

Note: Ghee stores indefinitely in a cool, dark place. Always use a clean dry spoon or knife when dipping into the ghee jar to protect it from moisture that can cause contamination. No refrigeration is required. In cool weather ghee remains in a solid form. In the warmer summer months ghee may take a liquid form.

ALLIUMS

Alliums include garlic, leeks, shallots, spring onions, green onions (scallions), and red, yellow, and white onions. These vegetables contain many potent natural substances that are good for the heart, cells, and immune system. The abundant polyphenols in alliums make them powerful antioxidants. The highest concentration of polyphenols are in the outer layers of their skins, so peel minimally. The quercetin that alliums contain gives them anti-inflammatory properties.

Because alliums bind flavors when cooked with other ingredients, they often serve as a basic component of stocks, soups, and stews. Peel, chop, and sauté until translucent in a small amount of oil or ghee. Fresh herbs and spices may be added while sautéing. For bean and lentil dishes, add alliums and seasonings at the end of cooking and then simmer for 5 minutes to allow their flavors to blend.

Traditional Japanese Seasonings

The number of centenarians living functional lives in Japan demonstrates how well the traditional Japanese diet promotes longevity. One reason is that the Japanese eat fermented foods like miso, natto, umeboshi plums, and pickled ginger daily. Other common Japanese seasonings include soy sauce, tamari, and wasabi. Japanese seasonings combined with Western herbs and spices can create unique flavors. Experiment to discover new combinations and expand your culinary choices.

Self-Healing
Medicinal Spices

Spices are some of the most nutrient-dense foods on our planet. The attributes they possess provide a natural pathway to healing. Some go as far as stimulating the production of antioxidants within the body, thus strengthening the body's own defense system. Furthermore, spices provide anti-inflammatory properties to improve gut health and prevent inflammation, one of the causes of chronic disease.

To learn more about the healing properties of spices, please refer to a book I highly recommend, *The Paleovedic Diet* by Dr. Akil Palanisamy, M.D. It offers further tips for greater health and was a valuable source for the content in this section.

In the following pages under the name of each spice, you will find their:

- Medicinal properties
- Culinary uses
- Safety profile and potential adverse effects

Ajwain*

- Supports respiratory system
- Benefits digestion
- Lowers blood pressure (extract)
- Protects liver (extract)
- Inhibits harmful bacteria and fungi in the intestines (essential oil)

Uses: Dry-roast seeds to soften their sharp flavor. Then grind into a powder and use in combination with other spices. A small amount is sufficient, as ajwain has an intense flavor. It goes well in curries and in vegetable and lentil dishes.

Safety profile: Excellent, no adverse reactions reported.

* Seeds can be purchased in Indian markets, some natural food stores, and online.

Allspice

- Antiviral and antibacterial
- High in antioxidants
- Relieves indigestion
- Lowers blood pressure by relaxing nervous system and improving blood flow
- May help regulate menstrual cycle
- May inhibit prostate cancer

Uses: Whole dried berries and powder forms are available. For maximum benefit, buy whole berries and grind them in a mortar and pestle before using. Allspice is versatile and good in both savory and sweet dishes. It blends well with other spices.

Safety profile: Excellent, no adverse reactions reported.

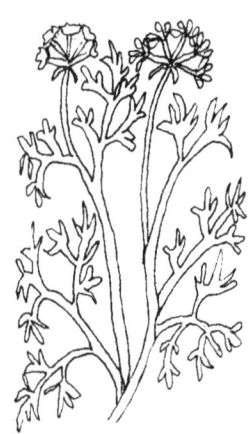
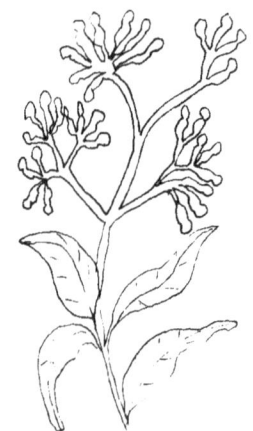

Black Cumin (Nigella sativa)*

- Antimicrobial
- Boosts the body's own antioxidant production
- Reduces inflammation
- Lowers blood pressure
- Normalizes blood sugar
- Decreases harmful LDL cholesterol
- Supports fertility in men

Uses: Use whole seeds liberally. Its mild peppery, aromatic flavor is good with vegetables and beans and in soups and sauces.

Safety profile: Use as a whole seed is very safe, although it is not recommended as a supplement during pregnancy because animal studies have shown that it can inhibit or prevent uterine contractions.

* Found in specialty food stores, online, and in Indian markets (as Nigella sativa or kolonji).

Cinnamon

- Antimicrobial
- High in antioxidants
- Normalizes cholesterol
- Lowers blood sugar
- Reduces inflammation
- Inhibits fungi (Candida albicans)

Uses: Cinnamon bark and powder forms are available. It's good in both savory and sweet dishes. Add to smoothies, breakfast cereals, baked goods, and hot beverages. (page 95)

Safety profile: Good in small quantities. To prevent any potential side effects, limit consumption of cinnamon cassia (commonly found in the supermarket) to 1 teaspoon per day. If large quantities are desired, seek out Ceylon cinnamon, which is found in specialty stores. As a spice, cinnamon is safe during pregnancy and breast feeding. However, as a supplement, avoid it because of possible adverse side effects.

Cloves

- Antimicrobial
- Good source of Vitamin K, fiber, and minerals'
- Has superior antioxidant potency
- Has remarkable anti-inflammatory markers
- Functions as an anesthesia for tooth aches and sore gums
- Heals anal fissures (topical clove oil cream)

Uses: Whole cloves have a longer shelf life and are the most potent. Roast whole cloves in a dry skillet over medium heat until fragrant and then grind them to a powder in a coffee grinder. Tasty in sweet and savory dishes. Add to curries, chili, beans, baked goods, and beverages.

Safety profile: Excellent, no adverse reactions reported.

Coriander

- Antimicrobial
- Potent antioxidant
- High in key phytochemicals
- Stimulates digestion
- Relieves gas and bloating
- Normalizes blood sugar
- Balances cholesterol

Uses: Buy coriander as whole seeds, which are good in soups and broths. Dry roast and grind seeds into powder for the richest flavor and to optimize health benefits. The powder is good in curries and vegetable sautés, and can be used liberally. When too much of another spice has been used adding coriander powder can help balance the flavor.

Safety profile: Generally safe, but avoid if allergic to cilantro. Buy organic to be safe because with non-organic coriander there is a risk of contamination with chemicals used in plastic manufacturing (phthalates).

Cumin

- Antibacterial (essential oil form)
- Potential to treat osteoporosis (liquid extract)
- Nutrient-dense
- Rich in antioxidant flavonoids
- Stimulates digestion
- Balances blood sugar
- Normalizes cholesterol
- May inhibit cancer

Uses: For maximum potency, buy whole cumin seeds, dry-roast, and grind into powder. Cumin seeds add aromatic flavor to vegetable and bean dishes. When preparing vegetable and rice dishes roast seeds in hot oil or ghee at the start of cooking.

Safety profile: Excellent, no adverse reactions reported.

Curry Leaf*

- Anti-inflammatory
- High in antioxidants
- Regulates blood sugar
- Supports memory and cognitive function
- May inhibit cancer

Uses: For maximum benefits, use fresh leaves rather than dried, and puree or finely chop leaves in combination with other spices. They can be stored in the refrigerator for up to a week or in the freezer for up to 3 months. Curry leaves are not the same as curry powder.

Safety profile: Excellent, no adverse reactions reported.

* Fresh curry leaves can be found in Indian markets, online, and stores in areas with a large Asian population.

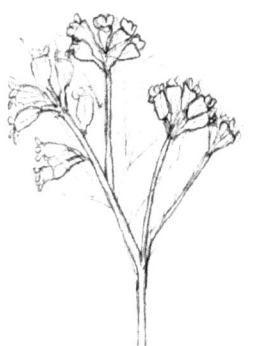

Fennel

- Anti-inflammatory
- A powerful antioxidant
- Strengthens digestion
- Relieves menstrual cramps (extract of fennel)
- May inhibit cancer

Uses: Fennel bulb, stalk, leaves, and seeds can all be used. Dry-roast seeds in a small amount of coconut oil or ghee at the beginning of cooking. Generously sprinkle seeds into soups, curries, and vegetable dishes. Fennel seeds can add a unique flavor to baked goods. See Hearty Soda Bread (pages 126-127)

Safety profile: Excellent, no adverse reactions reported.

Fenugreek (Trigonella foemun-graecum)

- Helpful in regulating blood sugar
- May lower cholesterol levels

Uses: Leaves, seed, and powder forms are available. Due to the hard exterior of the seeds they must be cooked well to make them more palatable. The powder form is more convenient and blends easily in cooking. Fenugreek adds a savory touch to curries and sautéed vegetables. A small amount is all that is needed.

Safety profile: Avoid if you suffer from allergies to peanuts, chickpeas, or coriander. Not advisable during pregnancy, as miscarriage or early labor could be triggered. Women with ovarian cancer or estrogen-dependent breasts should avoid fenugreek.

Ginger Root (Zingiber officinale)

- Anti-inflammatory
- Has potential to improve brain function
- Remedies nausea and gastrointestinal issues
- Fights infection
- Relieves cold and flu symptoms
- Helps prevent cancer

Uses: Fresh ginger root and powder form are readily available in most markets. Fresh ginger may be grated, chopped, or sliced and used to flavor a range of dishes, beverages, dressings, and sauces. The powdered form is milder in pungency and tasty in baked goods. Candied ginger can be used to sweeten beverages and desserts. Pickled ginger (page 220), commonly served with Japanese meals, is a fermented food.

Safety profile: Generally very safe as a spice; but large quantities may cause heartburn, diarrhea, or stomach upset. Those on blood-thinning medications should consult a physician before using as a supplement.

Saffron

- Anti-inflammatory
- A potent antioxidant
- Elevates mood
- Facilitates brain function (as extract)
- Relieves PMS
- Supports fertility

Uses: The stigma of the flower crocus sativa adds a distinctive yellow color to foods. Good in rice dishes and creamy desserts. Before cooking, soak saffron strands in water for 10 minutes so their volatile oils can be released. Do not soak in oil as this prevents the saffron oils from being released.

Safety profile: Excellent, no adverse reactions reported.

Turmeric

- Powerhouse of antioxidants
- Anti-inflammatory
- Reduces pain and swelling
- Facilitates brain function
- Helps treat disorders of the liver
- Prevents heart disease
- Protects against cancer

Uses: Both the root and the powder forms are beneficial. The addition of black pepper can increase the potency of tumeric by 2000 times. Tumeric may be added to almost any dish, as well as to beverages in modest amounts.

Safety profile: Excellent, no adverse reactions reported when used as a spice in food and beverages. Consult a physician before using as a supplement.

14 MENU PLANS

The most pleasing, satisfying meals are balanced in taste, texture, and color. Planned menus set you up for success, save time, and make preparation more efficient. These 14 thematic menu plans show you recipes from this cookbook that go together well.

	Page
French Vegetarian	70
Celebrate Springtime	71
Middle Eastern Vegan	72
Ayurvedic Dining	73
Time for Italian	74
Soothing & Balancing	75
Nourishing & Gratifying	76
Summer Freshness	77
Entertaining Friends	78
Warm-up in Winter	79
A Taste Of Spain	80
Simple & Substantial	81
Essential Nourishment	82
Fiesta Platter	83

MENU 1

French Vegetarian

> Oven-Roasted Cherry Tomatoes with Fresh Herbs (page 213)
>
> Lemon-Butter Roasted Cauliflower (page 189)
>
> Steamed Carrots (below)

This is a light, colorful meal. Start with the cherry tomatoes, as they take the longest to cook. Once the tomatoes are in the oven, steam the cauliflower, then transfer to a baking dish. Set aside the pan and steamer for the carrots. Reserve the water from the cauliflower for steaming the carrots. After the tomatoes cook for 15 minutes, place the cauliflower in the oven alongside the tomatoes.

Slice 4 carrots into 1/2 inch (1cm) rounds. Be sure there is at least 1 inch (5 cm) of liquid in the bottom of the steamer. Place the sliced carrots in the steamer and cover. About 10 minutes before the tomatoes and cauliflower are done, steam the carrots. and cook for 8 minutes or until tender.

If the tomatoes are done before the cauliflower, remove them from the oven and cover to keep warm. Serve on warmed plates. Pour the juice from the roasting pan of the cauliflower over the carrots. Add salt to taste. Garnish the carrots with finely chopped fresh cilantro or parsley.

MENU 2

Celebrate Springtime

> Red and Gold Beet Yogurt Salad (page 147)
>
> Swiss Chard-Portobellos Topped with Goat Cheese (page 175)
>
> Steamed Asparagus (below)

The beet salad can be made earlier in the day and stored in the refrigerator. Prepare the Portobellos and bake them in the pre-heated oven. Cook the asparagus about 5 minutes before the mushrooms are done.

Steamed Asparagus: Rinse well. Hold the root end in one hand and bend the spear end down with the other hand. It will break at the point between the tough and tender parts. Place the tender spears in the bottom of a large frying pan, and add about 1/2 inch (12 mm) water. Cover and bring to a simmer over medium-high heat. Remove from heat and let stand for 1 or 2 minutes, depending on the thickness of asparagus. Then pour water off and leave covered in pan for 2 more minutes. Before serving, add a few drops of lemon juice and drizzle with olive oil. Salt and pepper to taste.

Note: Compost tough stalks or use for soup broth.

MENU 3

Middle Eastern Vegan

> Cannellini Bean Hummus (pages 124-125)
>
> Quinoa Tabbouleh (pages 152-153)
>
> Blanched Rainbow Chard with Pine Nuts (page 180)

Start by cooking the Cannellini beans. I choose to cook beans in a pressure cooker as it shortens cooking time. Prepare the taboulleh while the beans are cooking. The taboulleh is more flavorful when it is allowed to stand for an hour before serving. The chard can be prepared closer to serving time.

Tip: Make and eat everything the same day to maximize nutritional value and to enjoy the fullest flavor.

MENU 4

Ayurvedic Dining

> Date-Mint Chutney (page 211)
>
> Healing Mung Bean Soup (pages 142-143)
>
> Millet-Basmati Pilaf (pages 158-159)

Start with the chutney in the morning or the night before. Store it in a tightly-closed glass jar in the refrigerator until you start cooking the soup and pilaf. To make the mung beans more digestible, you may want to soak them for an hour before cooking. Follow the instructions in the recipes given. Start cooking the pilaf 15 minutes after the beans start to boil, so both dishes will be done at the same time. The soup can also be made earlier in the day and reheated just before the pilaf is ready.

MENU 5

Time for Italian

Pistachio Pesto over Pasta (page 206)
with Oven-Roasted Tomatoes (page 213)

Marinated Green Bean Red Onion Salad (pages 154-155)

Almond-Cardamom Macaroons (page 194)

Enjoy this flavorful and visually appealing meal any time of the year. The pesto sauce can be made in the morning and kept in the refrigerator. About 40 minutes before cooking the pasta, remove the pesto from the refrigerator and set aside to bring it to room temperature. Prepare the Oven-Roasted Tomatoes to place in the oven 30 to 40 minutes before pasta is done. Check package directions for the timing of the pasta. The salad and macaroons can be made earlier in the day.

MENU 6

Soothing & Balancing

> Parsley-Mint Chutney (page 212)
>
> Split Red Lentils and Basmati Rice (pages 162-163)
>
> Steamed Seasonal Vegetables (below)

This calming meal is recommended when coping with excessive stress. You can make the chutney in the morning and the rice dish just before mealtime. Alternatively, you can make the rice dish in a rice cooker; and while it's cooking, prepare the chutney. Steam the seasonal vegetable just before the lentils and rice main dish are done.

Note: When you prepare the rice and lentils in a rice cooker, you'll have to sauté the spices in a skillet on the side and then add to the rice cooker with the lentils and rice.

MENU 7
Nourishing & Gratifying

> Roasted Zucchini with Onions and Tomatoes (below)
> Shiitake Mushroom Sauté (page 115)
>   with Leeks and Beet Greens added (below)

This easy to prepare 2-dish meal combines complementary flavors and textures with visual appeal. It may be enjoyed for breakfast, lunch, or dinner.

An hour before mealtime or earlier in the day, rinse and coarsely chop 3 to 4 medium-sized zucchini and 3 large tomatoes. Peel and cut 2 medium-sized red or yellow onions into 8 half-moon slices. Place the vegetables in a baking dish, add your favorite fresh or dried herbs and a dash of salt, drizzle with olive oil, and toss using 2 spoons to coat evenly. Preheat the oven to 350°F (180°C). Bake uncovered for 30 minutes and toss vegetables halfway through to insure even cooking.

While the zucchini dish is in the oven, chop the mushrooms, leeks, and beet greens for the sauté. Keep in mind the mushroom sauté takes 10 to 12 minutes. Follow the recipe for Shiitake Mushroom Sauté, substituting 2 medium-sized leeks (white and light green parts only) for the onions and adding the 2 cups chopped beet greens when the mushrooms begin to soften.

Note: I like the beet greens for the added nutritional value and support of liver function. Alternatively, Swiss chard or spinach may be substituted for the beet greens.

MENU 8

Summer Freshness

> **Mint-Cucumber Salad** (pages 150-151)
>
> **Spaghetti with Garlic-Basil Tomato Sauce**
> (pages 160-161)

This menu is best served in July and August when tomatoes are their most flavorful. The tomatoes for this sauce are left uncooked. The sauce is warming because of the garlic. The Cucumber-Mint Salad is cooling and balances the heat from the garlic in the sauce.

Make the salad earlier in the day, so the cucumbers can absorb the flavors of the marinade. Make the Garlic-Basil-Tomato sauce 1 hour before serving to allow the flavors to blend.

MENU 9

Entertaining Friends

> Puréed Parsnip-Celery Soup (page 144)
>
> Pecan Sun-Dried Tomato Torte
>   with Garlic-Lime-Yogurt Sauce (pages 164-165)
>
> Kale Confetti (page 188)
>
> Baked Sweet Potatoes with Ghee (page 190)

This menu requires about two hours of prep work, depending on how fast you chop. Make the soup earlier in the day and reheat before serving. Follow the torte recipe. Prep the sweet potatoes to go in the oven with the torte. If the sweet potatoes are large place them in the oven 10 to 15 minutes before the torte. While the torte is in the oven, prepare the Kale Confetti. If serving more than 4 people, you may want to cut and prep all the ingredients for the kale earlier in the day or the night before. Serve the soup as a starter and follow with other dishes.

MENU 10

Warm-Up in Winter

> Puréed Chickpea & Sun-Dried Tomato Soup (pages 134-135))
>
> Baked Spinach with Ground Pumpkin Seed Topping (page 181)
>
> Hearty Soda Bread (zucchini variation) (pages 126-127)

Make the soup first. Then prepare the spinach side. I like to make the bread close to serving time because it fills the kitchen with an appetizing aroma and tastes best right from the oven. The baked spinach takes 20 to 30 minutes, and the soda bread requires 30 minutes of baking time. Put them in the oven at about the same time. Then enjoy this great taste sensation!

MENU 11
A Taste Of Spain

> Puréed Spinach Soup (pages 136-137)
>
> Summer Saffron Paella (pages 166-167)

These recipes require lots of chopping. Start chopping ingredients early in the day or make it more fun by inviting friends to join you in the preparation. The soup can be made in the morning and reheated before serving it as a starter.

MENU 12

Simple & Substantial

> Miso-Barley Soup (pages 138-139)
> Garlic Toast (below)

This meal is good in cooler months when warm dishes are the most satisfying. Using a pressure cooker for the soup cuts the cooking time in half. The soup can be made in the morning and reheated right before serving.

Garlic Toast: Just before serving, toast 2 slices of bread, then rub them with a peeled and halved garlic clove. Drizzle olive oil over the garlic toast. If you prefer butter rather than olive oil, peel, crush or grate the garlic, wait 10 minutes, and then mix with softened butter.

Note: The 10-minute wait maximizes garlic's health-promoting qualities, giving its medicinal components time to develop.

MENU 13

Essential Nourishment

> Coconut-Cucumber-Cilantro Raita (page 210)
> Sweet-n-Spicy Adzuki Beans (pages 170-171)
> Steamed Short-Grain Brown Rice (below)

For greater efficiency make the raita in advance either the night before or the morning of serving. The beans can be cooked earlier in the day and reheated before serving.

Start the steamed Short-Grain Brown Rice about 40 minutes before serving the meal. Soak 1 cup (8oz/220g) rice for 30 to 40 minuters to remove arsenic. Rinse the rice and drain. In a 2-quart (1-l) saucepan, combine the rice, 2 cups (16/fl oz/500 ml) water, and 1/2 teaspoon salt. Bring to a boil over high heat, reduce the heat to low, cover, and simmer for 35 to 40 minutes, or until the water is completely absorbed and the rice is tender.

MENU 14
Fiesta Platter

> Three-Bean Salad with Sun-Dried Tomatoes (pages 148-149)
> Sautéed Zucchini and Spinach with Dill (page 182)
> Steamed Long-Grain Brown Rice (below)

Make the bean salad at least 1 hour or up to 4 hours ahead of time. A pressure cooker can cut the cooking time of the beans by half. The zucchini can be prepped while the beans are cooking. Time the cooking of the rice so that it will be ready when the zucchini and spinach are done.

Steamed Long-Grain Brown Rice: Soak 1 cup (8oz/220g) rice for 30 to 40 minuters to remove arsenic. Rinse the rice and drain. In 1-quart (1 l) saucepan, combine rice with 2 cups (16 fl oz/480 ml) water and 1/2 teaspoon salt. Bring to a boil over high heat. Then reduce the heat to low, cover, and simmer for 20 minutes or until the water is absorbed and the rice is tender.

Notes

TIMING
&
COOKING METHODS

Does your busy lifestyle leave you with limited time to prepare your own meals? Then this section may help you find cooking methods that suit the time you have available.

	Page
5-10 Minute Game Plans	86
10-20 Minute Game Plans	89
20-40 Minute Game Plans	91

5-10 MINUTE METHODS

Smoothies

Smoothies are best served in spring and summer for hydration and to up your intake of fruits and vegetables. Coarsely chop 1 cup (3 to 6 oz/90 to 185 g) fresh fruit or vegetables and add to a blender along with 1 cup (8 fl oz/250 ml) filtered water. Blend until smooth. For optimal digestion, avoid adding ice or frozen foods as iced beverages can inhibit digestion. (page 20)

Soup In A Blender

Coarsely chop 1 to 2 cups (3 to 6 oz/90 to 185 g) vegetables and add to a blender, then add about 1 1/2 cups (12 fl oz/375 ml) water or broth (page 132) and blend until smooth. For a thicker soup, add less liquid. Season to your taste with any combination of the following:

- a dash of salt and pepper
- a clove of crushed garlic
- grated fresh ginger
- a dash of ground cumin
- a dash of ground coriander
- combination of the above

When the soup is not heated, I add Vitamineral Green by HealthForce SuperFoods or spirilina to boost phytochemical intake. If I decide to heat the soup, I add sea vegetables instead of green powder because their nutritional value is not diminished by heat. One of my favorites additions is wakame. I take one teaspoon of dried wakame and immerse it in 3 tablespoons of water for 10 minutes. Then rinse and add to saucepan with vegetables and warm the soup over medium-low heat.

Serving Tips: For a more substantial meal, serve with seeded crackers topped with hummus and sliced avocado or your nut butter of choice.

Miso-Vegetable Soup

Simmer 1 cup (3 oz/90 g) shredded cabbage, 1 cup (5 oz/155 g) thinly sliced carrots, and 1/2 cup (2 1/2 oz/75 g) chopped green onions or leeks in 1 1/2 cups (12 fl oz/375 ml) water for 4 minutes or until tender. Meanwhile, whisk 1 tablespoon brown rice miso or mellow white miso in 1/2 cup (4 fl oz/125 ml) of water. When vegetables are tender, remove from heat and add the blended miso and serve.

<u>Variation</u>: Chopped kale, chard, or spinach may be substituted for cabbage. Simmer kale for 3 to 5 minutes, chard for 2 minutes, and spinach for 1 minute or less.

<u>Miso Vegetable Stew</u>: Follow the directions above, using less water and additional vegetables such as mushrooms, celery, or fennel root. Add 2 to 4 tablespoons of a quick-cooking grain like quinoa or millet, and cook for 12 to 15 minutes for a filling meal.

Serve with garlic toast (page 81) or your choice of energy nuggets (pages 120-123).

Spiralizing

Spiralizing is a way of cutting vegetables into linguini like strands which can be used in place of pasta and eaten raw, steamed, or sautéed. This offers an alternative to chopping.

Blanched Vegetable Salad

This makes an enjoyable lunch in summer and is a good source of protein. Bring a full pot of water to a rolling boil over high heat. Add a mixture of chopped vegetables that require the same amount of cooking time, such as carrots, green beans, and fennel root. When the water returns to a rolling boil, continue cooking for 2 to 4 minutes, without lowering the heat. Remove with a slotted spoon or pour through a sieve. Run under cold water or immerse in a bowl of ice water to stop the cooking.

<u>Note</u>: Shredded cabbage and chopped greens cook in 1 or 2 minutes. Blanching works well for cooked-vegetable salads, as it brightens the color of the vegetables and leaves them crunchy-tender. Dress with the nut butter sauce (page 88) to make the Indonesian salad, *Gado-Gado*.

Nut Butter Sauce

Put 1/4 cup (2 1/2 oz/75 g) almond butter, hazelnut butter, tahini (sesame paste), or any favorite nut or seed butter in a small bowl and add 6 tablespoons (3 fl oz/90 ml) vegetable cooking water, stirring in 2 tablespoons at a time to achieve a smooth consistency. Add 1/4 to 1/2 teaspoon curry powder and salt to taste. Warm the nut butter mixture in a small saucepan over low heat until the sauce thickens, about 2 minutes. If the sauce becomes too thick, slowly add 1 to 2 tablespoons water until desired consistency is achieved.

BE KITCHEN-EFFICIENT

- Save time in food prep by washing and chopping vegetables when you arrive home from the market.
- Store washed and chopped produce in closed containers so fresh-cut ingredients are ready to use at a moment's notice.
- Rinse, lightly dry, and chop fresh herbs in advance. Store in glass containers with lids. Use within 5 days. Cutting fresh herbs with scissors is faster and easier than chopping with a knife.
- Blend your favorite spice combinations in advance. Store in closed glass jars for use as needed.
- Measure out dry ingredients in advance for recipes you plan to make.
- Toast seeds and make healthy snacks over the weekend or in your free time. This can provide satisfying nourishment when hunger strikes.
- To shorten cooking time, use pans that have a wide-diameter bottom. The more surface area exposed to the heat source the faster the food will cook.
- When you cook, make an extra serving to enjoy again at dinner time or for lunch the next day.
- Keep your kitchen clean and organized. This creates an inviting place in which to cook and makes meal preparation more manageable.

10-20 MINUTE MEALS

Vegetable Sauté

Chop 2 cups seasonal vegetables. Heat 1 to 2 tablespoons ghee, sesame oil, or olive oil in a large skillet or wok over medium heat. Add the vegetables and stir constantly for 5 to 10 minutes, or until the vegetables are crisp-tender. The cooking time will depend on the vegetables you have chosen and whether they are chopped into rough or fine pieces. Serve over your favorite pasta or a whole grain, such as quinoa or brown rice. Top with some toasted sesame seeds, or pumpkin seeds. See Savory Seed Snack, page 130. Garnish with chopped parsley or cilantro.

Note: For an even faster sauté, shred the vegetables so they cook in 2 minutes. Add black or brown sesame seeds near the end of cooking to add a crunchy texture.

Steamed Vegetables

Steaming is a simple, low-calorie way to cook. Coarsely chopped green beans, spinach, and Swiss chard cook in 2 minutes or less. Root vegetables can take from 6 to 10 minutes depending on how finely they are chopped. Season steamed vegetables with salt and pepper to taste. Serve as a side dish or over rice, millet, or quinoa as a main dish. Drizzle with extra-virgin olive oil and 1/4 to 1/2 teaspoon freshly squeezed lemon juice. Garnish with dulse flakes, nori sheets cut into 1/2 inch (1 cm) squares, nuts, or toasted sunflower seeds for an added dimension of flavor and texture.

Quick-Cooking Grains With Vegetables

Cut vegetables into 3/4 inch (2 cm) bite-size pieces because if they are too small they will turn out mushy in cooking. In a medium saucepan, combine 1 cup (5 oz/150 g) chopped root vegetables such as carrots, parsnips, turnips with 1/2 cup (3 1/2 oz/105 g) quinoa, millet, or basmati rice. Add 1 cup (8 fl oz/250 ml) water, 1/4 teaspoon salt, 1/4 teaspoon ground turmeric, and a dash of freshly ground black pepper. Bring to a boil over medium-high heat. Then reduce the heat to low. Cover and simmer for 10 to 15 minutes or until the water is absorbed, the grain is cooked, and the vegetables are tender. Taste and adjust the seasoning and serve in a warmed bowl.

Pasta With Veggies

For this easy one-dish meal, select vegetables such as broccoli, carrots, and zucchini. Dice the carrots into small pieces and chop the zucchini and broccoli into chunky bite-size pieces. Cook pasta following the package directions. Add the vegetables to the cooking water about 4 minutes before the pasta is done. Drain the pasta and vegetables through a colander and then return to the pot. Add your favorite sauce or drizzle with olive oil, and toss to coat. Serve in warmed bowls and top with 1 tablespoon of nutritional yeast to add B vitamins and a richer flavor. Ground seeds, chopped nuts, or toasted nori are additional garnish options.

Sauté chopped mushrooms, onions, garlic, and fresh herbs such as parsley, thyme, oregano, basil, and marjoram in olive oil while the pasta is cooking. When the pasta is ready and mixed with the sauce, top with the sautéed vegetables and serve in warmed bowls..

20-40 MINUTE MEALS

Oven-Roasted Root Vegetables

Add coarsely chopped vegetables to a shallow baking dish or rimmed baking sheet lined with parchment paper. Season generously with fresh or dried thyme, basil, sage, marjoram, and oregano. Drizzle with olive oil, dust with salt, and mix with two large spoons. Roast for 30 to 40 minutes in a preheated 375°F (190°C) oven, stirring vegetables once during roasting for even cooking.

One-Dish Meals

One-dish meals or "bowls" can served up as a salad, a soup, or a rice and bean dish with veggies. For example, Miso-Barley Soup (page 138) and Split Red Lentils and Basmati Rice (page 162) are one-dish meals. Cooking foods together makes them more compatible with each other according to Ayurvedic principles. As a result, this kind of meal is easily digested.

Rice Cooker Combos

<u>12 to 15 minutes</u> cooking time: Try quinoa, white basmati rice, or millet with vegetables. I find sweet potatoes, butternut squash, and carrots work well. Stir in chopped chard or baby spinach when done to complete the meal.

<u>30 to 40 minutes</u> cooking time: Choose short-grain brown rice. After the rice has been cooking for 15 minutes, open the rice cooker and stir in the chopped vegetables. If your rice cooker has a steamer, add the chopped vegetables to the steamer and cook with the rice. Garnish either combo with nutritional yeast, seaweed flakes, toasted sesame seeds, or sunflower seeds.

Pressure-Cooked Meals

A pressure cooker can shorten cooking time by 50 to 70 per cent. Soups, stews, and bean dishes can be made in record time using a pressure cooker. Water-soluble vitamins and minerals are retained since less cooking liquid is required. Vegetables also retain more color and flavor. That is why I steam my artichokes in a pressure cooker. They always come out more flavorful.

For whole mung beans and adzuki beans allow 15 to 20 minutes. Black-eyed peas, navy, and pinto beans will take 30 to 40 minutes. Large, hard beans, such as black beans and chickpeas, will take 40 to 50 minutes. For about 3 cups (21 oz/655 g) cooked beans, use 1 cup (7 oz/ 220 g) beans in the pressure cooker and add water to cover by 1/2 to 1 inch (12 mm to 2.5 cm). About 5 to 7 minutes before beans are fully cooked, add vegetables, cut into 1/2 to 1 inch (12 mm to 2.5 cm) pieces. Basmati rice and quick cooking grains like quinoa may be added along with the vegetables. For safety, never fill the pressure cooker to more than half its capacity with grains, beans and legumes, as they tend to expand and froth during cooking. Soaking beans overnight make them more digestible and shortens cooking time even more.

<u>Sautéed seasonings for added flavor</u>: While beans are cooking, heat 1 tablespoon ghee or olive oil in a small frying pan until medium hot. Then add 1/2 to 1 teaspoon each of cumin and mustard seeds and a shake of asafoetida. When seeds pop, add a large clove garlic chopped and 1/2 inch (1cm) chopped fresh ginger root. Sauté for 1 to 2 minutes or until golden. Stir in 1/2 teaspoon ground turmeric and a 1/3 cup (1/2 oz/15g) fresh cilantro and remove from heat. When beans are tender, add the sautéed seasonings and simmer uncovered for 3 minutes allowing flavors to blend. Turn off heat and stir in chopped fresh greens such as spinach or Swiss chard, if desired. Salt and pepper to taste and serve.

<u>Variation</u>: If desired, chopped onions may be added along with the garlic and ginger.

Toaster Ovens

A toaster oven is a healthy alternative to a microwave. Toaster ovens are a convenient energy-efficient way to heat food in small portions.

RECIPES

My inspiration for these recipes comes from the kitchens of local cooks in Kyoto, Japan, the Mediterranean region of France, and rural northeastern Brazil. Spending time with local culinary artisans, I gained insights into ingredients and preparation methods that boost vitality and promote longevity.

I hope you enjoy expanding your culinary repertoire as you prepare and share these special plant-based dishes with your loved ones!

 Vegan    Gluten Free

GET READY TO FOLLOW A RECIPE

- Read the entire recipe first.

- Gather all the ingredients listed in the recipe.

- Assemble mixing bowls, measuring cups and spoons, pans and utensils needed.

- Prep vegetables and fruit and measure out the ingredients. Keep the prepared ingredients in small bowls so they can be added easily while cooking.

Note: The recipes in this cookbook have been prepared on an electric stove top. If you have a gas range, cooking times may be shorter.

HEALING BEVERAGES

For these recipes you can take advantage of spices commonly found in your kitchen cupboard. The caffeine-free beverages in this section are curative and balancing. Some aid digestion. Others support a healthy microbiome. Most are soothing and calming. For a good night's sleep, try Sweet Dreams.

	Page
Ginger Herbal Tea	96
Ginger-Cinnamon-Cardamom Breakfast Tea	97
Fennel-Cumin-Coriander Tea	98
Chamomile-Fennel-Cinnamon Tea	99
Mint Chai	100
Sweet Dreams	101
Mineralization Herbal Tea	102
Plain Lassi	103
Sweet Spiced Lassi	104

CURE
A COLD

Ginger Herbal Tea   Serves 4

Fresh ginger simmered in water makes a healthful beverage that can be sipped throughout the day. It is warming in cooler months and stimulates digestive juices. Ginger tea can serve as a base for coffee and teas, as well as cold drinks such as lemonade.

5 cups (40 fl oz/1.25 l) water
2 inches (5 cm) fresh ginger, peeled and thinly sliced

In a medium saucepan, bring the water to a boil. Add the ginger and reduce the heat to a simmer. Cover and simmer for 5 to 10 minutes, depending on the desired strength. Strain into a thermos or pitcher and serve.

<u>1 cup serving</u>: Grate 1/4 teaspoon fresh ginger into 1 cup (8 fl oz/250 ml) boiled water and let stand for 1 to 2 minutes.

<u>Medicinal qualities</u>: Ginger is known as the "universal medicine," as it treats a variety of ailments. Ginger has a heating quality and is traditionally used in Ayurveda to kindle digestive fire. This tea is said to improve circulation and is a good home remedy for coughs and colds. To soothe a sore throat, add 1/2 teaspoon raw honey to cooled tea. To cure a cold, add some lemon juice and a dash of cayenne pepper. This combination helps to break up congestion.

BRIGHTEN
YOUR DAY

Ginger-Cinnamon-Cardamom Breakfast Tea

Serves 2

Ignite your digestive fire with this mildly spicy beverage. It's good with cooked cereal such as oatmeal. This and the following 3 recipes come from Usha Lad and Dr. Vasant Lad's *Ayurvedic Cooking for Self-Healing*.

2 cups (16 fl oz/500 ml) water

1 teaspoon peeled and grated fresh ginger

1 teaspoon ground cinnamon

2 pinches ground cardamom

Sweeten to taste, if desired

In a small saucepan, bring the water to a boil. Stir in the spices and steep for 2 minutes. Add milk and sweeten as desired.

SAVORY
LIGHT REFRESHMENT

Fennel-Cumin-Coriander Tea Serves 2

This easy-to-make beverage can add a refreshing touch to your mid-day meal. It may be served warm or at room temperature. Try it with Quinoa Taboulleh Salad (pages 152-153) or Split Red Lentils & Basmati Rice (pages 162-163).

2 cups (16 fl oz/500 ml) water

2/3 teaspoon fennel seeds

2/3 teaspoon cumin seeds

2/3 teaspoon coriander seeds

In a small saucepan, bring the water to a boil and add spices. Remove from the heat and let steep for 2 minutes. Strain and serve warm or at room temperature.

RELAX
ENJOY YOUR EVENING

Chamomile-Fennel-Cinnamon Tea

Serves 2

This warming, soothing tea is best served in the evening. This is a pleasing drink to serve guests who prefer nonalcoholic beverages. Combines well with Sautéed Sweet Potatoes, Kale, and Walnut over steamed brown rice (pages 172-173).

2 cups (16 fl oz/500 ml) water

2/3 teaspoon dried chamomile

1/4 teaspoon fennel seeds

2/3 teaspoon ground cinnamon

In a small saucepan, bring the water to a boil. Add the spices and remove from heat. Steep for 2 minutes, strain, and serve warm or at room temperature.

ENLIVEN
THE SENSES

Mint Chai (Caffeine-free) — Serves 2 or 3

This flavorful aromatic spice combination makes the perfect afternoon tea. Try it as a substitute for dessert. For best results, use fresh mint when available.

- 3 cups (24 fl oz/750 ml) water
- 1/2 teaspoon grated or finely chopped peeled fresh ginger
- 3 pinches ground ginger
- 3 pinches ground cardamom
- 1 stick cinnamon
- 2 pinches freshly grated nutmeg
- 1 teaspoon coriander seeds
- 1 teaspoon cumin seeds
- 3 cloves
- 1/2 cup (1/2 oz/15 g) lightly packed fresh mint leaves, or 1 1/2 teaspoons dried mint
- 1 cup (8 fl oz/250 ml) raw organic whole cow's milk
- Sweeten with natural sweetener or 1 drop of Stevia

In a medium saucepan, bring the water to a boil and then add all the remaining ingredients. Reduce the heat to medium low and simmer for 2 to 3 minutes. Strain and serve. Sweeten as desired.

Note: If substituting with a nut milk, do not simmer with the other ingredients as nut milk can coagulate when simmered. Add near the end of simmering. Sweetening with honey is not advised when served warm. See Honey (page 225)

SLEEP
DEEPLY

Sweet Dreams
Serves 2

This comforting and calming spiced milk from Ayurvedic practitioner Ivy Amar relieves insomnia and deepens sleep. The spices in this recipe build stamina and boost the immune system.

2 cups (16 fl oz/500 ml) raw organic whole cow's milk

2 cups (16 fl oz/500 ml) water

7 to 8 slices fresh ginger

4 to 5 crushed cardamom pods

1/4 teaspoon ground cinnamon

1/4 teaspoon freshly grated nutmeg

2 to 4 strands saffron

1/4 teaspoon ghee (page 57), optional

4 almonds, crushed

1/2 to 1 teaspoon maple syrup, rice syrup, or 2 drops liquid stevia to sweeten

In a medium saucepan, combine all the ingredients except for the almonds and sweetener. Bring to a simmer over low heat, stirring occasionally, and cook for 20 to 30 minutes to reduce to 2 cups (16 fl oz/500 ml). Strain into a pitcher and add the almonds and sweeten as desired. Serve warm.

Note: Sweetening with honey is not advised. See Honey (page 225)

STRENGTHEN
BONES

Mineralization Herbal Tea

Makes 4 1/2 cups (4 1/2 oz/110 g) herbal blend

This herbal combination is a powerhouse of minerals that can strengthen and repair bones and support skin, hair, nail, and dental health. Drinking 2 cups (16 fl oz/500 ml) of tea made with this blend daily will provide you with significant amounts of silica, iron, calcium, magnesium, phosphorus, and potassium. In addition, studies have shown that these herbs have an ability to detoxify the body. They can be found in the bulk section of natural foods stores and online. This mineralization blend was given to me by Rupam, owner of Rupam's Herbals.   www.Rupamherbals.com

Herbal Blend

1/2 oz/10 g dried horsetail

1 oz/25 g each dried nettle, oat straw, red clover, and spearmint

In a large bowl, combine all of the herbs and mix thoroughly. Store the mixture in a glass jar with an airtight lid for up to 6 months.

To Brew

The night before serving, put 1 rounded tablespoon of the herbal blend in a glass jar. Gradually pour 2 cups (16 fl oz/500 ml) boiling water over the herbs, close the container, and let the herbs steep overnight. The next morning, strain the infusion and enjoy throughout the day. To mend a broken bone, drink 4 cups (32 fl oz/1 l) of this infusion a day.

PROMOTE
A HEALTHY MICROBIOME

Plain Lassi

Serves 2 to 3

This Indian yogurt drink promotes a healthy intestinal balance when taken 30 to 40 minutes after a meal. Ayurvedic practitioners say yogurt should only be consumed in a diluted form, as by itself, it is heavy to digest and can be mucus forming.

1 cup (8 oz/250 g) whole-milk organic yogurt or coconut yogurt

1 cup (8 fl oz/250 ml) filtered water

Combine the ingredients in a blender and blend on high speed or shake vigorously in a closed jar for 1 to 2 minutes.

Variations: For a savory lassi, add a little salt. For a sweet lassi, add a drop or two of stevia or a teaspoon of the natural sweetener of your choice.

LOVE
YOUR BODY

Sweet Spiced Lassi
Serves 3 to 4

The fresh ginger warms the body and aids digestion while the cardamom has a cooling affect with an exotic flavor. This combination makes a healthful substitute for dessert.

2 Medjool dates, pitted and quartered or 2 teaspoons raw honey, maple syrup, or 2 drops liquid stevia

1 cup (8 fl oz/250 ml) filtered water

1 cup (8 fl oz/250 ml) organic whole-milk yogurt or coconut yogurt

1/4 teaspoon freshly grated ginger

Dash of ground cardamom

If the dates are not moist, soften them by heating the water for the lassi in a saucepan, adding the dates, and letting them stand for 5 minutes or soak overnight. Drain, reserving the water. Combine the yogurt, ginger, cardamom, and dates in a blender. Blend to break up the dates and mix the ingredients. Add the reserved water and blend on high speed or shake vigorously in a closed jar for 1 to 2 minutes.

<u>Variations</u>: Add 1/4 teaspoon ground cumin or 1/4 teaspoon ground coriander or a combination of the two to the above ingredients, or to substitute for the ginger and cardamom. A dash of ground clove and cinnamon give this lassi a flavor that is reminiscent of chai.

COLD-PRESSED COFFEE
Makes 1 cup (8 fl oz/250 ml)

This recipe is from Café Gratitude, a raw-food restaurant in California. They say that this method of preparation lowers coffee's acidity by 80 percent.

1/2 cup (35 g) dark-roast organic coffee beans
1 1/2 cups (12 fl oz/375 ml) water

Grind the beans finely. Combine the ground beans and water in a French press and stir to break up any chunks. Let stand at room temperature for 24 to 48 hours; the longer it stands, the stronger the coffee will be. Press the coffee through the French press.

Dilute the concentrate with an equal amount of water. Heat gently over low heat for hot coffee. Add milk, if desired.

Note: According to Dr. Vasant Lad, Director of the Ayurvedic Institute, adding a pinch of ground ginger and cardamom to your coffee can neutralize the possible negative effect caffeine can have on the adrenal glands. Buying organic beans and grinding them fresh can prevent unnecessary consumption of added chemicals.

BREAKFAST

Eating a good breakfast eliminates cravings for sugary mid-morning snacks and provides sustained energy that can keep you going throughout the morning until your mid-day meal.

	Page
Bala Breakfast Condiment	108
Cream of Amaranth	109
Spiced Winter Squash Muffins	110
Grain-Free Almond, Pecan, Walnut Granola	112
Cinnamon Oatmeal with Toasted Coconut	114
Shiitake Mushroom Sauté	115
Buckwheat-Beet Pancakes	116
Sweet Coconut-Cardamom Basmati Rice	117

BUILD DIGESTIVE
POWER

Bala
Breakfast Condiment

Serves 2

Bala is a Sanskrit word meaning "strength." This condiment can be added to cooked cereal and spread on toast or crackers. It is delicately sweet and cooling. This recipe comes from Ivy Amar, an Ayurvedic practitioner.

12 raw organic almonds

1 tablespoon plus 1 teaspoon fennel seeds

2 teaspoons cardamom seeds (28 to 30 pods)

6 Medjool dates, pitted and diced

Put the almonds, fennel seeds, and cardamom seeds in a small bowl. Add water to cover by an inch and soak overnight.

In the morning strain the seed mixture through a fine-mesh sieve. Add to a mini food processor or blender with the dates and blend to a paste. Store in a sealed glass jar in the refrigerator for up to 7 days. Add a tablespoon or so to your cereal before serving. For a quick energy boost try a spoon or two on its own.

Note: The dates in *bala* breakfast add a natural sweetness, eliminating the need for other sweeteners. In Ayurvedic healing, this combination rejuvenates the nervous system.

IMPROVE
LUNG FUNCTION

Cream of Amaranth

Serves 2

Amaranth is an ancient gluten-free, nutrient-dense grain that is exceptionally high in the amino acid lysine. Amaranth is nutty in taste with a texture similar to cream of wheat.

3 cups (24 fl oz/750 ml) water

2/3 cup (4 1/2 oz/140 g) amaranth

1/4 teaspoon of salt

1/2 teaspoon ghee (page 57), optional

Rice syrup or maple syrup to taste or 3 to 4 drops liquid stevia

In a small saucepan, combine the water, amaranth, and salt. Bring to a boil, then turn heat to low, cover, and simmer for 25 to 30 minutes or until most of the water is absorbed and the consistency is creamy. Serve hot, topped with ghee and sweetened with rice syrup or maple syrup.

Variations: For a richer flavor, substitute almond, coconut, or oat milk for the water. To sweeten, add 2 finely chopped and pitted medjool dates or 1 tablespoon of the Bala Breakfast Condiment (page 108). For a thicker consistency, add 2 tablespoons almond butter. Garnish with toasted, sliced almonds.

HAVE
A JOYFUL DAY

Spiced Winter Squash Muffins

Makes 6 muffins

Honey nut and sweet bread winter squash, as the names imply, have a natural sweetness making these muffins a breakfast treat or a nutritious afternoon snack. The spices add subtle layers of flavor that enhance their natural sweetness.

- 1 lb (450 g) honey nut or sweet bread winter squash
- 1 1/4 cup (6 oz/170 g) pastry flour or gluten-free oat flour
- 1 1/2 teaspoon baking powder
- 1/2 teaspoon salt
- 1/2 teaspoon ground cardamom
- 1/2 teaspoon ground cinnamon
- 1/4 teaspoon ground ginger
- 1/4 teaspoon freshly ground allspice
- 1/4 teaspoon freshly ground nutmeg
- 1/4 cup (2 fl oz/60 ml) olive oil
- 1/4 cup (2 fl oz/60 ml)) maple syrup

Preheat oven to 325°F (170 °C) and line a baking pan with parchment paper.

Halve squash, remove seeds, and place face down on baking pan. Bake for 45 to 60 minutes or until the skin begins to brown and the squash is soft to a light touch. Remove from oven and set aside to cool and turn oven to 350°F (180°C)

While squash is cooling, whisk the dry ingredients together in a medium bowl.

When the squash has cooled, spoon out 2/3 cup (3 1/4 oz/80 g) squash from its skin and place in a large mixing bowl. Then add olive oil and maple syrup. With a hand mixer or wooden spoon, mix ingredients to a smooth consistency until no lumps remain. Then add the dry ingredients and mix with a rubber spatula until fully incorporated. Spoon into lined baking cups in muffin tin.

Bake for 25 to 30 minutes turning half way through baking. Place on a cooling rack for 10 to 15 minutes Remove from muffin tin and serve. May be stored wrapped in foil for up to 2 days.

Variations: 1/3 cup (50 g) chopped pumpkin seeds or pecans (35 g) may be added for more texture. Top with a few whole pumpkin seeds or one pecan before placing in oven. Other varieties of winter squash may be substituted if honey nut or sweet bread winter squash are not available.

Note: Excess squash from baking may be made into a base for a sauce or served as a puréed vegetable side or.

WAKE UP
AND ENERGIZE

Grain-Free Almond, Pecan, Walnut Granola

Makes 5 cups (20 oz/625 g)

The bonus to making your own granola is that you can control the amount of sweetener, and avoid processed oils and trans fats. I often enjoy this granola as a snack or as a desert with almond milk..

1/2 cup (2 oz/60 g) chopped walnuts
1 cup (4 oz/125 g) chopped almonds
1/2 cup (2 oz/60 g) chopped pecans
3/4 cup (3 oz/90 g) hulled sunflower seeds
1/2 cup (2 oz/60 g) hulled pumpkin seeds, ground or chopped
1/2 cup (2 oz/60 g) brown sesame seeds
1/2 cup (2 oz/60 g) black sesame seeds
1/4 cup (1 1/2 oz/45 g) dried figs, apricots, or dates, pitted and chopped
1/4 teaspoon salt
1 teaspoon ground cinnamon
1/2 teaspoon ground ginger
1/4 teaspoon ground cloves
1/4 cup (2 fl oz/60 ml) molasses or maple syrup (optional)
1/4 cup (2 fl oz/60 ml) coconut oil or ghee

Preheat the oven to 325°F (170°C) and line a rimmed baking sheet with parchment paper.

In a large bowl, combine all the ingredients except the molasses and oil and mix well. Spread the mixture evenly in a baking sheet. In a small pan, melt the coconut oil and then stir in the molasses and blend together. Drizzle the molasses and oil evenly over the nut and seed mixture, then mix together with two wooden spoons until evenly coated.

Bake for 10 minutes, then remove from the oven and stir. Return to the oven for 10 minutes or until fragrant and lightly toasted. Let cool completely. Store in an airtight glass container in the refrigerator for up to a month.

<u>Variations</u>: Barley flakes, rolled oats, or spelt flakes may be substituted for or in addition to nuts. If on a sugar-free diet, eliminate the molasses and sweeten with a few drops of stevia or some granulated xylitol when served.

BALANCE
AND NOURISH

Cinnamon Oatmeal with Toasted Coconut

Serves 2

The toasted coconut adds a nutty flavor and a bit of texture to this traditional porridge. This recipe is from *A Life of Balance* by Maya Tiwari. This porridge is a favorite with children, accordng to my friends with family.

1/4 cup (1 oz/30 g) shredded unsweetened coconut

1 cup (8 fl oz/250 ml) unsweetened almond milk

1 cup (8 fl oz/250 ml) water

3/4 cup (2 oz/60 g) rolled (old-fashioned) oats

1/4 teaspoon ground cinnamon

1/4 teaspoon ground turmeric

Dash of salt

1/2 to 1 teaspoon maple syrup or 2 drops stevia to taste

In a skillet over medium heat, dry toast the coconut for 2 to 3 minutes or until golden, stirring constantly; set aside. In a medium saucepan, bring the milk and water to boil, then add the oats and coconut. Stir in the cinnamon, tumeric, and salt, reduce the heat to low, and simmer uncovered for 8 minutes or until the oats are soft and consistency is smooth. Serve hot with maple syrup.

POWER UP

Shiitake Mushroom Sauté   Serves 4

The onions add a crunchy texture and the mushrooms an earthy flavor, while the ginger and cayenne add a touch of pungency. This is a tasty substitute for scrambled eggs and makes a satisfying dinner with a seasonal vegetable. (see menu plan page 76)

One 14-ounce (440 g) package firm organic tofu

2 to 3 tablespoons ghee (page 57) or sesame oil

1/2 red onion, finely chopped

4 ounces (125 g) shiitake mushrooms, stemmed and sliced

1 teaspoon peeled and chopped fresh ginger

1 teaspoon ground turmeric

1/3 cup (1/2 oz/15 g) chopped fresh cilantro or parsley

Dash of cayenne pepper

1/2 teaspoon salt

Crumble the tofu into a bowl. In a medium skillet, melt the ghee over medium heat. Add the onion and mushrooms and sauté for about 2 minutes or until tender. Add the ginger, turmeric, cilantro, cayenne, and salt, and sauté for 1 minute, stirring to mix well. Add the tofu and stir for 1 to 2 minutes. Reduce the heat to low and simmer for 7 to 10 minutes, stirring occasionally. Taste and adjust the seasoning. Serve hot on warmed plates.

<u>Variations</u>: Three eggs may be substituted for the tofu in this recipe. Chopped Swiss chard, or spinach may also be added.

TREAT
YOURSELF

Buckwheat-Beet Pancakes

Makes about 18 3 1/2-inch (9-cm) pancakes

Here's a tasty way to get some veggies in your morning meal. The beets turn these pancakes pink, making them visually appealing to children.

1 cup (5 oz/155 g) buckwheat flour
1 teaspoon aluminum-free baking powder
1 teaspoon coconut palm sugar
1/2 teaspoon ground cinnamon
1/4 teaspoon ground coriander
1/4 teaspoon salt
1 cup (8 fl oz/250 ml) unsweetened nut milk or organic whole milk
1 egg
1 tablespoon olive oil or ghee
1/2 cup (2 oz/60 ml) grated raw beets
Ghee (page 57) or butter and maple syrup for serving

In a medium bowl, stir all the dry ingredients together. In a small bowl, whisk the milk, egg, and sesame oil until smooth. Stir in the grated beets. Stir the beet mixture into the dry ingredients with a fork and blend until smooth.

Heat a large nonstick skillet over medium heat. When pan is hot, pour about 1/8 cup (1 fl oz/30 ml) batter into the pan for each pancake, spacing them so they don't touch. When tiny bubbles appear on the surface, turn the pancakes over and cook for 1 to 2 minutes on the other side or until lightly browned. Serve with ghee and maple syrup on warmed plates.

TAKE A
CULINARY JOURNEY

Sweet Coconut-Cardamom Basmati Rice

Serves 2

Ignite the senses with the aromatic flavors of the coconut and cardamom in this easy-to-make rice dish. The inspiration for this breakfast comes from the exotic flavors of South East Asian cuisine. Serve warm, garnished with cilantro.

1/2 teaspoon cardamom seeds (from about 8 cardamom pods)

1 cup (7 oz/220 g) white basmati rice

2 cups (16 fl oz/500 ml) coconut milk (page 220)

1/4 teaspoon salt

4 Medjool dates, pitted and chopped

1 teaspoon ghee (page 57), optional

2 tablespoons minced fresh cilantro

In a medium saucepan, combine the rice, cardamom, coconut milk, salt, and dates and bring to a boil. Reduce the heat to low, cover, and simmer for 10 minutes or until rice is tender. Turn off the heat, stir in the ghee to enrich the flavor, cover, and let stand for 5 minutes.

Variations: Add 1 teaspoon minced candied ginger to cook with rice. Garnish with toasted coconut instead of cilantro. May be served as an afternoon snack or dessert.

Notes

SNACKS & APPETIZERS

Healthful snacks can provide nourishment when hunger arises between meals. The recipes in this section are nutrient-dense and can tide you over until your next meal.

	Page
Almond Butter Nuggets	121
Sprouted Cinnamon Nuggets	122
Hemp Seed Energy Nuggets	123
Cannellini Bean Hummus	124
Hearty Soda Bread	126
Ginger-Tumeric Sautéed Plantains	128
Spiced Molasses Walnuts	129
Savory Seed Snack	130

ENERGY NUGGETS

The following nuggets are a delicious, nutrient-dense alternative to store-bought "power" bars that typically contain highly processed oils, refined sugar, artificial sweeteners, and low-quality ingredients.

EMPOWERING
NOURISHMENT

Almond Butter Nuggets

Makes 20 walnut-sized nuggets

These nuggets offer a high protein, essential fatty acid boost. The almond butter adds richness and the walnuts and cacao nibs provide texture.

1/3 cup (1 1/2 oz/45 g) chopped walnuts

1/3 cup (1 1/2 oz/45 g) ground brown or black sesame seeds

1/3 cup (1 1/2 oz/45 g) cacao nibs

3/4 cup (7 oz/220 g) almond butter

2 Medjool dates, pitted and chopped

1/8 teaspoon salt

1 teaspoon vanilla extract

1/4 cup nutritional yeast or ground sesame seeds for coating

In a medium bowl, combine all the ingredients except the nutritional yeast and stir to blend. Roll by tablespoonfuls into walnut-sized balls. Place nutritional yeast in a small bowl and roll the nuggets in nutritional yeast to coat. Store in an airtight container in the refrigerator for up to 2 weeks.

Note: If the nut butter is runny, add nutritional yeast to thicken the mixture and hold the ingredients together. Finely ground sunflower seeds can also be used for thickening.

RISE UP
AND REVITALIZE

Sprouted Cinnamon Nuggets

Makes 20 walnut-sized nuggets

Lydia's "Sprouted Cinnamon Cereal" makes these nuggets truly unique. A friend describes them as a healthy version of "Ferrero Rocher" chocolates. The sprouted cinnamon cereal can be found in some natural food stores or ordered online.

1 cup (4 1/2 oz/125 g) Lydia's Sprouted Cinnamon Cereal

1/2 cup (5 oz/155 g) almond butter

2 tablespoons raw honey

1/8 teaspoon salt

1 teaspoon vanilla extract

1/4 to 1/3 cup (1 to 1-1/2 oz/30 to 45 g) nutritional yeast or ground sesame seeds for coating

In a medium bowl, combine all the ingredients except the nutritional yeast. Stir to blend. Roll into walnut-sized balls. Place the nutritional yeast in a small, shallow bowl and roll the nuggets in it to coat. Store in the refrigerator in an airtight container for up to 2 weeks.

Note: If the nut butter is runny, add nutritional yeast to thicken and hold the ingredients together. Ground sesame or sunflower seeds can be used for thickening as well.

Variations: Hazelnut butter or another nut butter may be substituted for the almond butter. Coarsely grind a combination of your favorite nuts and seeds in a blender to substitute for the cereal. The almond grounds from almond milk (page 219) work well as a substitute for Lydia's "Sprouted Cinnamon Cereal" and make this snack gluten-free.

ELEVATE
OMEGA-3 INTAKE

Hemp Seed Energy Nuggets

Makes 10 walnut-sized nuggets

The hemp and flax seeds offer a good dose of omega-3 and can keep you going when your body calls for nourishment. This highly nutritious snack can also serve as a dessert after a meal.

- 3/4 cup (3 oz/90 g) ground hemp
- 1/4 cup (1 oz/30 g) ground flaxseeds
- 1/8 teaspoon salt
- 1/4 teaspoon ground cinnamon
- 1/4 teaspoon ground cardamom
- 1 tablespoon coconut oil or ghee
- 2 tablespoons tahini (sesame paste)
- 1 tablespoon raw honey
- 1/2 teaspoon vanilla extract
- 2 or 3 drops liquid stevia (optional)
- 1/4 cup (1 oz/30 g) ground sesame seeds for coating

In a medium bowl, combine all the ingredients except the ground sesame seeds and stir to blend. Roll by tablespoonfuls into walnut-sized balls. Put the ground sesame seeds in a shallow bowl and roll the balls in ground seeds to coat. Store in an airtight container in the refrigerator for up to 2 weeks.

SATISFYING
AND VERSATILE

Cannellini Bean Hummus

Makes 2 cups (24 oz/750 g)

This nourishing spread is tasty on crackers and toasted pita bread, and it's also great as a party dip with crudités. For wraps, spread thinly and add a mixture of sprouts and baby greens.

1 cup (7 oz/220 g) dried cannellini beans

1/3 cup (3 oz/90 g) tahini (sesame paste)

1/4 cup (2 fl oz/125 ml) fresh lemon juice

1/2 teaspoon ground coriander

1/4 teaspoon ground cumin

1 clove garlic, crushed

1/4 cup (2 fl oz/60 ml) extra-virgin olive oil

1/2 teaspoon salt

1 to 4 tablespoons (2 fl oz/60 ml) water as needed

Pick over the beans to remove small stones and dirt particles. RInse, then soak in water to cover by 2 inches (5 cm) overnight. Drain and rinse the beans.

Put the beans in a large pot with 2 inches (5 cm) water to cover. Bring to a boil over medium-high heat, then reduce the heat to medium-low. Simmer uncovered for 1 to 1 1/2 hours or until tender, stirring occasionally and adding water as needed to keep the beans submerged. Drain.

In a blender, combine the tahini, lemon juice, coriander, cumin, garlic, oil, and salt and purée. Add the beans and mix until smooth, stopping the blender to push the beans down as needed. If the hummus is too thick to blend, add water a tablespoon at a time.

Pressure Cooker Method: To save 20 minutes in cooking time, rinse and soak the beans as in main recipe. Combine the beans and water in a 4-quart (4-l) pressure cooker. Close and lock the pressure cooker. Bring to full pressure, turn the heat to low, and cook for 25 to 30 minutes. Proceed with the main recipe.

Variations: Hummus can be made with almost any beans, cooked carrots or beets can be added in the blending process to boost micronutrients, add color, and vary the flavor. For a "fresh from the garden" flavor, replace the cumin and coriander with a 1/3 cup (1/2 oz/15 g) combination of finely chopped fresh rosemary, marjoram, and thyme.

CRUSTY
GOODNESS

Hearty Soda Bread

Makes 6 4-inch (10 cm) rounds

Michele Schultz, an Ayurvedic cook, gave me this recipe. This easy-to-make bread is crusty, dense, and yeast-free. Fresh from the oven, it makes a tasty snack spread with ghee or nut butter. It can be sliced, toasted, and then topped with sliced avocado.

3 1/2 cups (18 oz/560 g) unbleached spelt, whole-wheat, or gluten-free flour

2 tablespoons organic sugar

1 teaspoon baking soda

1 teaspoon aluminum-free baking powder

1/2 teaspoon sea salt

2 teaspoons fennel seeds

1 1/2 cups (7 oz/220 g) shredded carrots

1 cup (8 fl oz/250 ml) plain whole-milk kefir, almond milk, or water

2 tablespoons melted ghee (page 57) or olive oil

3/4 cup (3 oz/90 g) chopped walnuts (optional)

Preheat the oven to 350°F (180°C). Line baking sheet with parchment paper.

In a large bowl, combine all the dry ingredients and the fennel seeds. In a medium bowl, combine the carrots and kefir, then stir in the ghee and walnuts. Add the wet ingredients to the dry ingredients and mix with a fork until fully incorporated. The dough should be moist and sticky. If too wet, add flour 1 tablespoonful at a time. If too dry, add water 1 tablespoonful at a time.

To keep dough from sticking to your hands, rub oil generously over them before you start shaping the loaves. Then form the dough into 6 rounds, each about 1 inch (2.5 cm) high and 4 inches (10 cm) in diameter and place on the prepared baking sheet. Bake for 30 minutes until the tops of the loaves are slightly golden. Remove from oven and place on a cutting board. Cut in half top to bottom, then slice each half vertically. Serve warm. Wrap leftover bread in a clean tea towel and store at room temperature as refrigeration tends to dry breads out. To enjoy later, warm slices in a toaster or toaster oven. Soda bread will keep for up to 2 days.

<u>Variations</u>: Shredded zucchini may be substituted for the shredded carrots. For a sweeter variation, substitute shredded sweet potato for shredded carrots. If including nuts, substitute chopped pecans for chopped walnuts with sweet potato version.

SAVORY
AND SATISFYING

Ginger-Turmeric Sautéed Plantains

Serves 2

Sautéed green plantains are a tasty snack that can satisfy a craving for packaged chips. An added plus is that plantains are a prebiotic food that can nourish health-promoting microbes in the intestinal tract. I like to make this recipe for breakfast once or twice a week.

2 tablespoons sesame oil

2 green plantains, peeled, cut crosswise into thirds, and thinly sliced lengthwise

Salt and freshly ground black pepper to taste

2 inches (5 cm) fresh ginger, peeled and finely chopped

2 inches (5 cm) fresh tumeric root (curcumin), peeled and finely chopped

1/2 cup (2/3 oz/20 g) chopped fresh cilantro

Fresh lemon juice or lime juice for sprinkling

Salt and pepper to taste

In a large skillet, heat 1 tablespoon of the oil over medium heat until hot. In batches, add the plantains in one layer. Add a dash of salt and pepper. Cook for 2 to 3 minutes on one side or until underside is golden. Turn and add the ginger, curcumin, and cilantro. Cook for 2 minutes or until golden. Using a slotted metal spatula, transfer to paper towels to drain and top with another paper towel. Repeat until all the slices have been cooked, adding more oil to the pan as needed.

Remove from the paper towels and serve warm sprinkled with lemon or lime juice.

LIFT SPIRITS
WITH SWEETNESS

Spiced Molasses Walnuts

Makes 1 cup (4 oz /125 g)

This recipe is an easy-to-make treat. These sweet spiced walnuts can add a tantalizing contrast to a salad of arugula or other bitter greens. As a garnish, they can add a crunchy accent to cakes, muffins, and puddings, except for chocolate as their flavors tend to compete.

2 tablespoons molasses

1/2 cup (4 fl oz/125 ml) water

1/2 teaspoon ground cumin

1/2 teaspoon ground coriander

1/4 teaspoon ground turmeric

Dash of cayenne pepper

1 cup (4 oz/125 g) organic, raw, unsalted walnuts

In a small bowl, stir together the molasses, water, and spices. In a medium skillet, bring the molasses mixture to a simmer over medium heat. Add the walnuts and cook, stirring constantly, until the liquid evaporates and coats the nuts. Take care not to burn. Remove from the heat, transfer to a plate, and let cool. Store in a glass jar for up to 2 weeks.

Note: If glazed walnuts are sticky to the touch when cool, transfer to a rimmed baking sheet and place in a preheated 375°F (190°C) oven for 7 to 10 minutes. Allow to cool before storing.

PERK UP
THE TASTE BUDS

Savory Seed Snack

Makes 1 cup

The cumin-coriander combo with tamari adds a warm savory flavor. Enjoy these seeds as a snack or sprinkle over salads or cooked grains for added crunch and protein.

1/2 teaspoon ground cumin

1 teaspoon ground coriander

1 tablespoon tamari or coco aminos

3 tablespoons water

1 cup (5 oz/145 g) raw sunflower seeds

Preheat oven to 400 °F (200 °C). Line a sided baking sheet with parchment paper. In a medium bowl, combine the cumin, coriander, tamari, and water. Add the sunflower seeds to the bowl and stir to coat seeds evenly with spice mixture. Spread evenly on a sided baking sheet or baking dish. Bake for 10 to 12 minutes, then remove from the oven, stir, and return to oven for an additional 5 to 7 minutes or until liquid has evaporated and the seeds are toasted. Remove from oven, stir, and let cool. Store in an airtight glass jar in a cool, dark place for up to 2 weeks.

Variation: Pumpkin seeds may be substituted for sunflower seeds. Proceed with the main recipe. Bake for 15 minutes. After stirring return to the oven for an additional 10 to 15 minutes.

SOUPS

Please the palette, comfort the body, and warm the soul by trying a recipe in this section. They can keep you hydrated, support weight loss, and are a great way to add more vegetables to your diet. Soups are naturally healing, inexpensive, and easy to prepare. An added plus is that they offer a fun way to be creative in the kitchen.

	Page
Vegetable Broth	132
Vegetable Soup	133
Puréed Chickpea & Sun-Dried Tomato Soup	134
Puréed Spinach Soup	136
Miso-Barley Soup	138
Winter Squash Soup	140
Healing Mung Bean Soup	142
Puréed Parsnip-Celery Soup	144

A BASIC STARTER
FOR RICHER FLAVOR

Vegetable Broth

The secret of a good soup is a full-bodied broth. Easy to make and well worth the time taken to prepare.

Best Broth Ingredients: Celery leaves, onions, onion skins, pea pods, greens from leeks, peels and seeds from winter squash, carrots, carrot tops.

Herbs: Fresh parsley; sprigs of thyme; fresh rosemary, fresh marjoram; bay leaves.

Corn, Potatoes: Good for bulk, but they make the broth cloudy.

Beets: Add sweetness and impart a deep red color.

Note: Wilted vegetables can be used, but never anything that has mold or is spoiled.

Vegetables to avoid: Artichokes, cabbage, brussel sprouts, cauliflower, broccoli, kale, rutabagas, and turnips. They can overwhelm a broth with a bitter tint.

To make vegetable broth: Rinse the mixed vegetable cuttings and put them in a soup pot. Add cold water to cover by 2 or 3 inches. Bring to a boil over medium-high heat, then reduce to medium-low and simmer, partially covered, for 1 to 2 hours. The longer the broth simmers the more flavorful. Remove from the heat and allow to cool. Strain through a sieve into a bowl. Store in a closed glass jars in the refrigerator for up to 3 days. Taste before using, to make sure flavor is compatible with the ingredients in your recipe.

CLEANSE
AND NOURISH

Vegetable Soup
Serves 6

This soup is excellent to have when you feel a cold coming on. Enjoy it weekly to cleanse the body and prevent a build-up of toxins. It is alkaline-forming, nourishing, and light. The ingredients can be varied according to taste.

- 3 tablespoons sesame oil or ghee (page 57)
- 2 to 3 inches (5 to 7.5 cm) fresh ginger, peeled and minced
- 3 to 6 cloves garlic, minced
- 2 onions, chopped
- 3 cups (15 oz/470 g) diced seasonal vegetables
- 2 quarts (2 l) water or broth
- Freshly ground black pepper to taste
- Coco aminos or tamari sauce to taste

In a soup pot, melt the ghee over medium heat and sauté the ginger, garlic, and onions for 3 minutes, or until the onions are slightly translucent. Stir in the seasonal vegetables. Add the water and bring to a boil. Simmer for 15 to 20 minutes, or until the vegetables are tender. Before serving, add pepper and coco aminos to taste.

Variations: For an Asian flavor, garnish with cilantro, mung bean sprouts, and finely chopped green onions. For an Italian flavor, use olive oil and add 1 teaspoon dried basil, 1/2 teaspoon dried oregano, and 1/4 teaspoon dried thyme when sautéing the ginger, garlic, and onion. For an Indian flavor, add 1 teaspoon mustard seeds to the hot ghee and sauté until the seeds pop, and add 1/2 teaspoon each of ground cumin, coriander, and turmeric when sautéing the ginger, garlic, and onion.

HEARTY
& WARMING

Puréed Chickpea & Sun-Dried Tomato Soup

Serves 4

This thick soup is filling and comforting in winter. The cayenne pepper perks up the subtleness of the bay leaves and fresh rosemary. Try Menu 10 (page 79) for complete meal.

1 1/4 cups (9 oz/280 g) dried chickpeas

5 to 6 cups (40 to 48 fl oz/1.25 to 1.5 l) water

3 bay leaves

2 sprigs fresh rosemary

2 tablespoons oil-packed sun-dried tomatoes, drained and chopped

3 tablespoons olive oil

3 cloves garlic, chopped

1 red bell pepper, seeded, deveined, and chopped

Dash of cayenne pepper

1 teaspoon salt

Pick over the chickpeas to remove small stones and dirt particles. Rinse and soak overnight in water to cover by 2 inches (5 cm). The next morning drain and rinse the chickpeas.

Put the chickpeas in a large pot with the water. Using kitchen twine, tie the bay leaves and rosemary in a square of cheesecloth to make a *bouquet garni*. Bring the liquid to a rapid simmer over medium-high heat, then reduce the heat to medium-low. Cook uncovered for 1 to 1 1/2 hours or until the beans are tender, stirring occasionally and adding water as needed to keep them submerged.

In a medium skillet, heat the olive oil over medium heat, add the red pepper and sauté for 1 to 2 minutes or until the pepper starts to soften. Add the garlic and sauté for 1 minute or until it turns golden. Add the sun-dried tomatoes and cayenne. Sauté for 1 minute and remove from the heat.

When beans are done, remove the rosemary and bay leaves from the cooked beans. Stir in the sautéed mixture and add the salt. Simmer for 15 minutes over medium-low heat to blend flavors.

Purée the soup with an immersion blender or in small batches in a blender on low speed. Taste and adjust the seasoning. Return to the pot and warm over medium heat to serve.

Pressure Cooker Method: Rinse and soak the beans as in the main recipe. Combine the beans, 4 cups (32 fl oz/1 l) water, and *bouquet garni* in a 4-quart (4-l) pressure cooker. Close and lock the pressure cooker. Bring to full pressure, turn heat to low, and cook for 30 to 40 minutes. Proceed with the method in the main recipe.

Variation: 3 tablespoons of tomato paste may be substituted for the sun-dried tomatoes. Add the tomato paste to the sautéed garlic and red bell pepper just as you would the sun-dried tomatoes.

STEP FORWARD
WITH HEAVENLY GREEN

Puréed Spinach Soup

Serves 4

This nourishing soup is an excellent way to get a good dose of leafy greens. The rich color and creamy texture make it the perfect starter. According to Ayurvedic texts, spinach is good for asthma, as a decongestant, and as a blood builder.

2 pounds (1 kg) fresh spinach, stemmed and rinsed thoroughly

3 tablespoons extra-virgin olive oil

1 large onion, coarsely chopped

2 large cloves garlic, chopped

1/4 teaspoon freshly ground black pepper

1/4 teaspoon freshly grated nutmeg

5 cups (40 fl oz/1.21 l) broth or water

1 1/4 teaspoon salt

1/4 cup (1 oz/30 g) pine nuts, toasted (page 221)

4 lemon wedges

Blanch the spinach for 2 minutes in boiling water, drain, and rinse under cold water to refresh. Squeeze by handfuls to remove excess liquid. Chop coarsely.

In a large soup pot, heat the olive oil over medium heat and sauté the onion and garlic for 3 minutes or until the onion is translucent. Add the pepper and nutmeg and sauté for a few seconds. Add the spinach, broth, and salt to the pot. Bring to a boil, reduce the heat, and simmer gently, uncovered, for 5 minutes. If too watery, cook over high heat until the desired consistency is achieved and then purée in batches in a blender on low speed or with an immersion blender in the pot until creamy.

Serve warm, garnished with the pine nuts and with a slice of a lemon wedge on the side of the bowl.

<u>Variations</u>: A pinch of cayenne pepper may be added for a touch of pungency. Swiss chard can be substituted for the spinach.

LOW CALORIE
NOURISHMENT

Miso-Barley Soup   Serves 6

This soup makes a satisfying meal that is hearty and palate pleasing. The texture of the cooked barley adds a pleasing contrast to the chopped vegetables. Barley fans, this soup is for you.

1/2 cup (4 oz/125 g) hulled or pearl barley

3 quarts (3 l) water

2 tablespoons sesame oil

2 cups (8 oz/250 g) coarsely chopped onion

3/4 cup (3/1/2 oz/105 g) diced carrots

1 cup (2 oz/60 g) sliced celery

5 ounces (155 g) shiitake mushrooms, stemmed and thickly sliced

1 1/3 cups (4 oz/125 g) shredded cabbage, rinsed

1/2 cup (4 fl oz/125 g) brown rice miso

1/2 cup (4 fl oz/125 ml) cold water

1/4 cup (1/4 oz/7 g) minced fresh flat-leaf parsley

Rinse the barley twice. In a soup pot, combine the barley and water. Bring the water to a boil, then reduce the heat and simmer uncovered for 45 minutes.

Meanwhile, in a large skillet, melt the ghee over medium heat and sauté the onion and mushrooms for 3 to 5 minutes, or until onion is translucent and mushrooms have softened. Then add the carrots and celery and sauté for 3 minutes. Remove from the heat.

After the barley has simmered for 45 minutes, add the sautéed vegetables and simmer for 10 minutes or until the vegetables are tender. Add the cabbage and simmer for 3 minutes, or until the cabbage starts to soften. Turn off the heat.

In a small bowl, whisk the miso and water together and stir into the soup. Serve, garnished with parsley.

Pressure Cooker Method: Add the barley to a 4-quart (4-l) pressure cooker with 8 cups (64 fl oz/2 l) broth or water. Close and lock the pressure cooker. Bring to full pressure, then reduce the heat to low, and cook for 20 to 25 minutes, or until the barley is done. When the barley is done add the vegetables. Replace the lid and lock. Bring to full pressure, turn heat to low, and cook for 5 minutes. Release the pressure and check the vegetables. If tender, add the cabbage and continue with the above method.

Variations: Spelt or kamut can serve as a good alternative to barley. Short-grain brown rice makes a gluten-free version. For a milder flavor, substitute white or mellow miso for brown rice miso.

COMFORTING
ON A COLD DAY

Winter Squash Soup
Serves 4-6

The deep orange color of this filling soup brings sunshine to your table. The prominent ginger warms the body and soul. Serve as a starter or as the centerpiece of a meal with some steamed greens alongside and garlic toast. (page 81)

2 tablespoons olive oil or ghee (page 57)

2 onions, chopped

1 tablespoon peeled and finely grated fresh ginger

1/4 cup (1 1/2 oz/45 g) crystallized ginger, rinsed and chopped

1 1/2 teaspoons salt

2 pounds (500 g) butternut or other winter squash, peeled, seeded, and cut into 1/2-inch (12-mm) pieces.

5 cups (40 fl oz/1.2 l) broth or water

1 cup (6 fl oz/180 ml) coconut milk

Chopped fresh marjoram or cilantro, for garnish

In a medium soup pot, melt the ghee over medium heat. Add the onions, fresh ginger, crystallized ginger, and salt. Sauté until the onions are translucent, about 3 minutes. Stir in the squash, then add the broth and bring to a simmer. Cover, reduce the heat to medium-low, and cook until the squash is very tender, about 20 minutes.

Purée the soup with an immersion blender or in small batches in a blender. Return to the saucepan, stir in the coconut milk, and pass through a sieve into a bowl. Before serving, return to pan and heat gently over medium-low heat. Pour into soup bowls and garnish with fresh marjoram or cilantro.

Variation: Preheat oven to 325°F (170°C). Line a sided baking sheet with parchment paper. Halve squash, remove seeds, and place face down on baking sheet. Bake for 50 to 70 minutes or until skin starts to brown. When cool, spoon squash out from its skin. Add to sautéed onions and proceed with recipe method.

BLESS
YOUR BODY

Healing Mung Bean Soup   Serves 4

This soup nourishes all the tissues of the body and is given as a holistic remedy for indigestion in Ayurveda. Mung beans are one of the most alkaline legumes. Ivy Amar, an Ayurvedic practitioner, shared this recipe for well-being.

1 cup (7 oz/220 g) whole mung beans

8 cups (64 fl oz/2 l) water

2 tablespoons sesame oil or ghee (page 57)

2 to 3 teaspoons peeled and grated fresh ginger

2 or 3 tablespoons minced garlic

1 cup (1/3 oz/40 g) chopped fresh cilantro

1/4 teaspoon freshly ground black pepper

Coco aminos or tamari sauce to taste

Rinse the beans until the water runs clear. For better digestion, soak the beans covered by 2 inches of water for 30 minutes, drain and rinse.

In a soup pot, combine the water and mung beans. Bring to a boil, reduce the heat to medium, partially cover, and simmer over medium heat for 25 to 30 minutes, or until the beans are tender.

In a medium skillet, melt the ghee over medium heat. Add the ginger, garlic, and cilantro and sauté for 1 or 2 minutes. Add the sautéed mixture to the beans. Add the pepper and more water if necessary. Simmer for 5 minutes. Season to taste with Coco Liquid Aminos before serving.

Pressure Cooker Method: Combine the beans with 4 cups (32 fl oz/1 l) water in a 4-quart (4-l) pressure cooker. Close and lock the pressure cooker. Bring to full pressure, reduce the heat to low, and cook for 10 minutes. After 10 minutes, remove from heat, release the pressure, and remove lid. Sauté the spices and continue as directed above.

Variations: Assorted vegetables, such as carrots, celery, green beans, and fennel root can be added in the last 10 minutes of cooking. Add 1/3 cup (2 1/3 o/70 g) basmati rice, quinoa, or millet to the beans along with 1 cup (8 fl oz/250 ml) water to make this a filling, energizing meal.

DAIRY-FREE
CREAMY GOODNESS

Puréed Parsnip-Celery Soup

Serves 4

The parsnips give this soup a creamy consistency without the addition of cream. Before potatoes were brought to Europe from the New World, parsnips were commonly used to thicken soups. Their subtle sweetness contrasts well with the crunchy texture of the celery.

3 cups (15 oz/470 g) diced peeled parsnips

5 cups (40 fl oz/1.2 l) light-colored vegetable broth

1 tablespoon ghee (page 57) or butter

1 1/2 cups (9 oz/280 g) finely chopped celery

1/2 teaspoon salt

1/8 teaspoon ground white pepper

Chopped celery leaves for garnish

In a soup pot, combine parsnips and 4 cups (32 fl oz/1 l) broth. Bring to a boil, reduce the heat, cover, and simmer for 15 to 20 minutes, or until the parsnips are tender.

While the parsnips are cooking, melt the ghee in a medium saucepan, add the celery, and sauté for 1 or 2 minutes. Add 1 cup (8 fl oz/250 ml) broth and simmer for 7 or 8 minutes or until the celery is tender. Remove from the heat. Transfer the parsnips to a blender and purée on low speed. Return to the pot and add the celery with its cooking liquid, the salt, and pepper. Reheat if necessary and serve garnished with fresh celery leaves.

SALADS

Enjoy a salad at mealtime for a powerful punch of micronutrients. The high water content in raw vegetables and salad greens hydrates the cells and their dietary fiber supports digestive health. Garnish with seeds and nuts to add protein and essential fatty acids. The dressings included in these recipes are suitable for any salad.

	Page
Carrot-Jicama Salad with Candied Ginger	146
Red & Golden Beet Yogurt Salad	147
Three-Bean Salad with Sun-Dried Tomatoes	148
Mint-Cucumber Salad	150
Quinoa Tabbouleh	152
Marinated Green Bean & Red Onion Salad	154
Celery Salad with Lemon-Honey Dressing	156

CRUNCHY FRESH
SWEETNESS

Carrot-Jicama Salad with Candied Ginger

Serves 4-6

This salad is a delicious variation on the traditional carrot and raisin combo. The almond butter adds protein and the olive oil gives this crunchy salad a dose of balanced essential fatty acids as well as antioxidants. The candied ginger offers natural sweetness.

2 carrots, shredded

2 golden beets, peeled and shredded

2 jicamas, peeled and shredded

1 tablespoon finely chopped and rinsed candied ginger

1/3 cup (3 oz/90 g) almond butter

1/4 cup (2 fl oz/60 ml) extra-virgin olive oil

1/4 teaspoon salt

In a large bowl, combine the vegetables. Stir in the ginger.

In a small bowl, stir the almond butter, olive oil, and salt together until smooth. Add to the shredded vegetables and toss to coat. Taste and adjust the seasoning.

Variations: Add 1/4 cup (1 oz/30 g) toasted black or brown sesame seeds to boost essential fatty acids. Two chopped dates may be added or substituted for candied ginger. White carrots or parsnips may be substituted for jicama.

COLOR THE PLATE
WITH HARVEST HUES

Red & Golden Beet Yogurt Salad

Serves 4

The red and golden beets make a colorful presentation, and their natural sweetness creates a flavorful contrast served on a bed of fresh arugula.

---

2 red beets, stems trimmed to 2 inches (5 cm)

2 golden beets, stems trimmed to 2 inches (5cm)

1/2 cup (4 oz/125 g) coconut or whole milk yogurt

1/4 teaspoon salt, divided

2 cups (2 oz/60 g) arugula

Put the red beets in a medium saucepan and the golden beets in another, add water to cover each by 2 inches (5 cm). Bring the water to a boil over high heat, then reduce the heat to medium, and simmer uncovered for 40 minutes, or until a knife slides easily into the beets. Drain and place in separate bowls of cold water. When cool enough to handle, rub off the skins. Shred the red and golden beets into separate bowls. Add 1/4 cup (2 oz/60 g) of the yogurt, 1/8 teaspoon salt to each bowl, mix gently. Taste and adjust the seasoning.

Put the arugula in a large bowl, drizzle with olive oil, dust with salt and pepper, then toss to coat.

Place a bed of arugula on each of 4 salad plates. Using an ice cream scoop or a 1/4-cup (2 fl oz/60 ml) measuring cup, drop the red beets into the center of each plate. Then spoon one-fourth of the yellow beets around the red beets to form a ring and serve.

A TRIFECTA
OF NOURISHING PLEASURE

Three-Bean Salad with Sun-Dried Tomatoes

Serves 4-6

The sliced red onions and blanched green beans add the perfect crunch to this colorful summer salad. It's a real eye-catcher on picnic tables and at potlucks. Add 2 cups (14 oz/440 g) cooked short-grain brown rice for a complete one-dish meal.

1 cup (7 oz/220 g) cooked black beans

1 cup (7 oz/220 g) cooked chickpeas

1/2 cup (1 1/2 oz/45 g) thinly sliced red onion

2 tablespoons oil-packed sun-dried tomatoes, drained and finely chopped

8 ounces (250 g) green beans cut into 1-inch (2.5 cm) pieces

1/2 cup (2 oz/60 g) chopped green onion, including green parts

1 tablespoon maple syrup

2 tablespoons olive oil

2 tablespoons apple cider vinegar

3/4 teaspoon salt

1/4 teaspoon freshly ground black pepper

Put the black beans and chickpeas in a large salad bowl. Soak the red onions in salted water for 20 to 30 minutes to remove any bitterness. Then drain and rinse with cold water and add to the beans. Add the sun-dried tomatoes to the bowl of black beans and chickpeas.

In a large saucepan of boiling water, blanch the green beans for 1 to 2 minutes. Drain and place in a bowl of ice water to stop cooking. Drain again and add to the bowl of other ingredients. Add the green onions.

In a small bowl, whisk the maple syrup, olive oil, vinegar, salt, and pepper together. Pour over the beans and toss to coat. Cover and refrigerate for at least 1 hour or up to 3 hours, stirring occasionally.

Note: To avoid turning the chickpeas reddish brown, soak and cook the chickpeas separately from the black beans.

Variations: Add 1 minced garlic clove and 2 finely chopped celery stalks. Fresh lemon juice may be substituted for the vinegar.

COOL DOWN
IN SUMMER

Mint-Cucumber Salad
Serves 4

The cooling qualities of the cucumbers and mint make this salad a revitalizing side in summer weather. This salad pairs well with hot spicy dishes to balance and cool their pungency. The consistency of the mint-almond dressing is similar to pesto sauce.

Salad

2 cucumbers, peeled and sliced crosswise

Dressing

1 cup (1 1/2 oz/40 g) chopped fresh mint, reserving a sprig or two to garnish

2 cloves garlic, crushed

2 tablespoons raw almonds, blanched, peeled (page 219) and soaked overnight

1/2 cup (4 fl oz/125 ml) olive oil

2 tablespoons rice vinegar

Salt and freshly ground black pepper to taste

Put the cucumbers into a salad bowl.

For the dressing: In a small food processor or blender, process the mint, garlic, and almonds to make a paste. Add the olive oil and vinegar and pulse to blend. Add the salt and pepper.

Add the dressing to the cucumbers and toss to coat. Let stand in refrigerator for 45 to 60 minutes so the cucumbers can absorb the flavors. Taste and adjust the seasoning. Serve on a bed of salad greens. Garnish with 3 small mint leaves.

Variations: Lemon juice or apple cider vinegar may be substituted for the rice vinegar. One or two avocado slices may be added to garnish.

Spiralizer Variation: Cut the cucumbers crosswise into 4-inch (10 cm) lengths, remove the seeds from center with an apple corer or teaspoon, spiralize onto a large cutting board and cut the cucumber strands into 2-inch lengths, place the cut strands into the bowl, and toss with the dressing. Line a salad bowl with romaine lettuce leaves, fill the center with the cucumber spaghetti, and garnish with slices of avocado. A julienne peeler offers an additional option, the cucumber pieces will turn out similar in size to toothpicks.

GOING
ON A PICNIC

Quinoa Tabbouleh

Serves 6-7

This traditional Middle Eastern dish is usually made with bulgur or cracked wheat. Quinoa is gluten-free and contains all the essential amino acids for complete protein. This salad is terrific for picnics and potluck buffets and makes a nutritious lunch to take to work.

Salad

1 cup (5 oz/155 g) quinoa
3 green onions, finely chopped
1/4 cup (1/3 oz/10 g) chopped fresh flat-leaf parsley
1/4 cup (1/3 oz/10 g) chopped fresh mint
1/3 cup (3 oz/90 g) raw almonds, soaked for 8 hours and chopped
1/4 cup 1 1/2 oz/45 g) currants (optional)
1/3 cup (1 1/2 oz/45 g) diced carrot

Dressing

1/2 cup (4 fl oz/125 ml) extra-virgin olive oil
1 teaspoon raw honey
Juice of 1 lime
1 large clove garlic, minced
1/2 teaspoon ground cumin
Salt and freshly ground black pepper to taste
Red leaf lettuce leaves for serving

Rinse the quinoa, drain, and add to a 1-quart (1-l) saucepan with 2 cups (16 fl oz/500 ml) water and 1/2 teaspoon salt. Bring to a boil, reduce heat to low, and cover. Cook for 12 to 15 minutes, or until the water is absorbed and the grain is cooked. Let stand for 15 to 20 minutes uncovered to cool. In a salad bowl, combine the quinoa, green onions, parsley, mint, almonds, currants, and carrot.

For the dressing: In a small bowl, whisk the olive oil, honey, and lime juice together. Add the garlic, cumin, salt and pepper, and whisk to blend. Pour over the salad ingredients and mix. Let stand for 20 minutes to blend flavors.

Serve on a bed of red leaf lettuce. Garnish with finely chopped mint leaves, seaweed flakes, or toasted sesame seeds (page 221).

Note: 3 tablespoons fresh lemon juice may be substituted for the lime juice.

A GO-TO
COMPANION

Marinated Green Bean & Red Onion Salad

Serves 4

This salad can add a complementary touch to any meal. The contrast of the red onions with the green beans offers an appetizing temptation. Serve as a starter or a side.

Salad

1/2 small red onion, thinly sliced lengthwise

1/2 teaspoon salt

10 ounces (315 g) green beans, trimmed

Marinade

1/2 cup (4 fl oz/125 ml) olive oil

1/4 cup (2 fl oz/60 ml) fresh lemon juice

1 clove garlic, minced

1 1/2 teaspoons maple syrup

3/4 teaspoon fresh marjoram, or 1/4 teaspoon dried

3/4 teaspoon fresh thyme, or 1/4 teaspoon dried

3/4 teaspoon fresh basil, or 1/4 teaspoon dried

1/4 teaspoon salt

Freshly ground black pepper to taste

Put the onions in a small bowl and add water to cover by 1-inch, then add the salt and stir. Let stand for 30 to 60 minutes to remove any bitterness.

In a medium saucepan of salted boiling water, blanch the green beans for 2 minutes, or until crisp-tender. Drain and plunge the beans into a bowl of cold water with ice to stop them from cooking. Drain and dry on paper or tea towels and put into a square or rectangular dish about 2 inches (5 cm) deep.

For the marinade: In a small bowl, whisk all the ingredients together. Drain and rinse the onions, then add to the beans. Pour the marinade over the beans and onions. Cover and refrigerate for 1 hour, stirring once or twice.

Note: The marinade that is left after salad is served may be poured over steamed vegetables or used as a salad dressing on another occasion. The dressing may be stored in a glass jar in the refrigerator for up to 7 days.

LIGHT
& REFRESHING

Celery Salad with Lemon-Honey Dressing

Serves 4

The freshness of the crisp celery combined with the tart and tenderly sweet dressing is the perfect starter for a meal. The walnuts add contrast in taste and texture and are high in omega-3s.

Dressing
1 tablespoon fresh lemon juice
2 teaspoons raw honey
1 teaspoon mustard
3 tablespoons extra-virgin olive oil
Salt to taste
Freshly ground pepper to taste

Salad
2 cups (12 oz/375 g) finely chopped celery
1 cup (6 oz/185 g) shredded jicama
3 tablespoons walnuts, chopped
Red leaf or butter lettuce for serving

For the dressing: In a small bowl, combine all the ingredients and whisk until blended.

For the salad: In a medium bowl, combine the celery, jicama, and walnuts, reserving 1 tablespoon walnuts to garnish. Pour the dressing over the salad and toss to coat.

Serve on a leaf of butter lettuce. Garnish with reserved walnuts and freshly ground pepper.

Note: If jicama is not available, substitute with an additional cup (6 oz/185 g) celery.

MAIN DISHES

Some of the main dishes in this section can be served as a one-dish meal, while others are best combined with one or two sides. Choose sides that complement the main dish in color, taste, and texture. See Menu Plans for suggestions (pages 69 to 83).

	Page
Millet-Basmati Pilaf	158
Spaghetti with Garlic-Basil-Tomato Sauce	160
Split Red Lentils & Basmati Rice	162
Pecan Sun-Dried Tomato Torte with Garlic-Lime-Yogurt Sauce	164
Summer Saffron Paella	166
Black Bean Mushroom Patties	168
Sweet-n-Spicy Adzuki Beans	170
Sautéed Sweet Potato, Kale & Walnuts over Brown RIce	172
Swiss Chard-Portobellos Topped with Goat Cheese	175
Brown Rice Pasta with Broccoli & Umeboshi Plums	176

COLORFUL
& PORTABLE

Millet-Basmati Pilaf
Serves 4

The contrasting colors of the carrots, spinach, and golden millet make this a vibrant, visually appealing dish. This was adapted from a recipe by Ayurvedic cook Michelle Schultz. For picnics or a lunch to go, this pilaf can be cooled and wrapped in sheets of nori to make California rolls. The millet retains an al dente texture as a result of toasting.

3/4 cup (4 oz/125 g) millet

1 cup (7 oz/220 g) white basmati rice

1/2 teaspoon cumin seeds

3 1/2 cups (28 fl oz/790 g/875 ml) water

1 1/4 teaspoon salt

2 medium carrots, diced, about 3/4 cup (8.5 oz/100 g)

2 small zucchini cut in half-moons, 1/4 inch (6 mm) thick

2 tablespoons fresh lime juice

1/4 cup (2 fl oz/55 g/60 ml) extra-virgin olive oil

1/2 teaspoon ground turmeric

2 cups (4 oz/125 g) chopped spinach leaves

3 tablespoons minced fresh basil

1/4 cup (1 oz/30 g) sunflower seeds, toasted (page 221)

In a sieve, rinse the grains together until the water runs clear and drain. In a dry medium skillet over medium heat, stir the millet, basmati, and cumin seeds until the seeds pop.

Add the grains and water to a 4-quart saucepan and bring to a boil over high heat. Add the salt and carrots, reduce the heat to low, cover, and simmer for 6 to 7 minutes. Then check the grains to see if the water is evaporating quickly. If so, add 2 to 5 tablespoons water, as needed.

Add the zucchini and push down into the grains with the back of a wooden spoon, cover and cook for 7 to 8 minutes more or until water is absorbed and the grains are cooked.

While the grains are cooking, whisk the lime juice, olive oil, and turmeric together in a small bowl. When the grains are cooked, stir in the spinach, basil, and turmeric mixture. Taste and adjust the seasoning. Serve warm, garnished with the toasted sunflower seeds.

Variations: Lemon juice may be substituted for lime juice. Fresh mint leaves may be substituted for the basil. For a richer taste, 2 cups (8 fl oz/250 ml) coconut milk (page 220) may be substituted for 2 cups (8 fl oz/250 ml) of water. Garnish with toasted coconut or micro-greens.

To make a nori wrap: Place a nori sheet shiny side down on a work surface and, beginning with the end of the sheet toward you, spread a 1/2 inch (12 mm) layer of pilaf over about two-thirds of the sheet. Begin rolling the nori sheet tightly until you reach the uncovered last third. Brush the last inch of the sheet with water or umeboshi paste and finish rolling the sheet, pressing the moistened last inch closed to seal the wrap. Using a sharp knife cut the nori wrap into bite size pieces.

ADD SOME SUNSHINE
TO YOUR PLATE

Spaghetti with Garlic-Basil-Tomato Sauce

Serves 4

Garlic lovers, this dish is for you! The fresh tomatoes and basil absorb the garlic flavor well and give a potent kick to the sauce. Serve in the summer when tomatoes and basil are in season, for lunch or a light supper.

Sauce

2 pounds (1 kg) tomatoes, peeled, seeded, and chopped (pages 220-221)
4 to 6 garlic cloves, crushed
1 cup (1 1/2 oz/45 g) lightly packed fresh basil leaves before chopping
1/4 cup (2 fl oz/60 ml) extra-virgin olive oil
Salt and freshly ground black pepper to taste

Pasta

1 pound (500 g) spaghetti
1 tablespoon extra-virgin olive oil
3 zucchini, cut into 1/2-inch (12-mm) rounds
Freshly ground black pepper to taste

For the sauce: Mash the tomatoes with a fork in a shallow bowl until smooth. Pour into a medium bowl. Crush the garlic and basil in a mortar with a pestle or in a mini food processor to make a paste. Add the basil mixture to the tomatoes. Pour in the olive oil and add salt and pepper to taste. Mix well and let stand for 20 minutes to blend flavors before serving.

Cook the pasta in a large pot of salted boiling water until al dente. Refer to the package directions for approximate cooking time.

While the pasta is cooking, heat the olive oil in a large skillet over medium heat, and sauté the zucchini for 3 minutes on each side, or until golden. Using a slotted spatula, transfer to paper towels to drain.

Drain the pasta and divide it evenly among 4 warmed pasta bowls. Top with the tomato sauce, then the zucchini and freshly ground pepper.

Spiralizer Variation: If you're on a low-carb diet and want to avoid pasta, use a spiralizer to make zoodles, aka zucchini spaghetti. Spiralize 2 zucchini per person, serve as is, and top with tomato sauce or sauté in olive oil for about 2 minutes, just enough to warm without losing the crunch. Toss with tomato sauce, sprinkle with freshly ground pepper, and serve.

CALM
MIND, BODY, AND SPIRIT

Split Red Lentils & Basmati Rice

Serves 4

To relieve stress try this Ayurvedic one-dish meal known as *kitchari*. The combination of spices and ingredients is soothing and comforting. This dish is adapted from a recipe in *Ayurvedic Cooking for Self-Healing*, by Usha Lad and Dr. Vasant Lad.

1 cup (7 oz/220 g) split red lentils

1 cup (7 oz/220 g) basmati rice

2-inch (5-cm) piece fresh ginger, peeled and finely chopped

2 tablespoons unsweetened shredded coconut

1/3 cup (1/2 oz/15 g) chopped fresh cilantro

1/2 cup water

3 tablespoons ghee (page 57) or olive oil

Two 1 1/2-inch (4-cm) pieces cinnamon stick

8 cloves

8 green cardamom pods

10 black peppercorns

6 bay leaves

1 teaspoon ground turmeric

1 teaspoon salt

4 1/2 cups (36 fl oz/1.1 l) boiling water

1 cup (5 oz/155 g) peeled and diced butternut squash

Rinse the lentils and rice separately twice. Soak for 30 minutes for better digestion, if time allows. After soaking, rinse in a sieve until the water runs clear.

In a blender, combine the ginger, coconut, cilantro, and 1/2 cup (4 fl oz/125 ml) water and purée. In a large saucepan, melt the ghee over medium-low heat, then add the cinnamon, cloves, cardamom, peppercorns, and bay leaves and sauté for about a minute, or until fragrant.

Add the ginger mixture to the saucepan and then add the turmeric and salt. Stir for about 5 minutes or until the mixture turns lightly browned. Add the lentils and rice and mix until well coated with spices. Add the boiling water. Bring to a boil over medium-high heat and cook for 5 minutes. Reduce the heat to low, cover, and simmer for 15 minutes. Add the butternut squash and re-cover. Cook another 10 to 15 minutes, or until the lentils and rice are tender and most of the liquid has been absorbed; the consistency will be slightly soupy. Taste and adjust the seasoning. Serve warm.

Pressure Cooker Method: Follow the above method, using a 4-quart (4-l) pressure cooker. Add the squash to the pot with the lentils and rice. Bring to full pressure over high heat, then reduce the heat to low, and cook under pressure for 15 minutes. To avoid overcooking, remove from heat, release the pressure, and open the pot to check if the lentils and rice are tender. If not, cook 5 more minutes under pressure.

Rice Cooker Method: Follow the above method, using a medium-size saucepan to sauté the spices. Add the rice, lentils, and squash to the skillet and sauté for 1 or 2 minutes to coat all of the ingredients with the spices. Spoon all of the ingredients into the rice cooker and add water and salt. Cover and turn on the cooker.

Variation: Carrots or sweet potato may be substituted for the butternut squash.

Note: Parsley-Mint Chutney (page 212) is a tasty condiment with this dish.

EXPLORE
FLAVOR SENSATIONS

Pecan Sun-Dried Tomato Torte with Garlic-Lime-Yogurt Sauce
Serves 4-6

The flavors of the sun-dried tomatoes and pecans are absorbed beautifully by the rice, adding richness to this hearty dish. The quick and easy garlic-lime sauce makes this torte a real winner. The preparation of this dish takes some time, but once the torte is in the oven, the cook is free to entertain guests and do other tasks.

Sauce
1 clove garlic, crushed

Juice of 1 lime

1 cup (8 oz/250 g) whole-milk yogurt

Dash of salt

Torte
1 1/2 cups (12 fl oz/340 g/375 ml) water

3/4 cup (5 oz/155 g) short-grain brown rice, rinsed

1 small russet potato, peeled and cubed

1/2 teaspoon salt

2 tablespoons extra-virgin olive oil

1 cup (4 oz/125 g) coarsely chopped onion

1 cup (5 oz/150 g) shredded carrot

1 1/2 teaspoons fresh thyme or 1/2 teaspoon dried thyme

1 1/2 teaspoons finely chopped fresh rosemary or 1/2 teaspoon dried

1/4 teaspoon paprika

5 oil-packed sun-dried tomatoes, drained and finely chopped

1 cup (4 oz/125 g) chopped pecans

1/2 teaspoon salt

1/4 teaspoon freshly ground black pepper

<u>For the sauce</u>: In a small bowl, combine all of the ingredients and stir until smooth. Transfer to a serving dish.

<u>For the torte</u>: In a large saucepan, bring the water to a boil over high heat. Rinse the rice and potato, drain, add to boiling water and cook uncovered for 5 minutes, then reduce the heat to low, cover, and cook for 35 to 40 minutes, or until the water is absorbed and the rice is tender.

Preheat the oven to 375°F (190°C). Oil a 9-inch (23-cm) cake or pie pan.

In a large skillet, heat the olive oil over medium heat. Add the onion and sauté for 2 to 3 minutes or until translucent. Add the carrot, herbs, and paprika and sauté for 1 or 2 minutes or until carrots soften. Stir in the sun-dried tomatoes, sauté for 1 minute, then remove from the heat.

When the rice is cooked, put it in a large bowl and mash with a potato masher or fork to a mushy consistency, leaving some texture to the rice. Stir in the sautéed vegetables, pecans, salt, pepper, and mix well. Taste and adjust seasoning.

Spread the mixture evenly in the prepared pan, cover with aluminum foil, and bake on the center rack of the oven for 25 minutes. Uncover and continue baking for 30 to 35 minutes, or until lightly browned. Remove from the oven. Cut into wedges and serve with the yogurt sauce.

<u>Vegan version</u>: Substitute coconut yogurt for whole-milk yogurt.

HAVE
A PARTY

Summer Saffron Paella
Serves 4

This vegan version of this celebrated Spanish dish sets the stage for a lively atmosphere in the kitchen. Perfect for inviting friends to share in the preparation fun.

2 pinches saffron threads

3 cups (24 fl oz/225 g750 ml) plus 1 tablespoon water

1 1/4 cups (9 oz/280 g) long-grain brown rice

6 tablespoons (3 fl oz/85 g/90 ml) olive oil

1/4 teaspoon ground turmeric

1/2 teaspoon salt

1/2 cup (2 1/2 oz/75 g) green peas or cubed carrot

1 small yellow bell pepper, seeded, deveined, and chopped

1 small red bell pepper, seeded, deveined, and chopped

2 zucchini, cubed

2 onions, sliced lengthwise

3 tomatoes, peeled, seeded, and chopped (pages 220-221)

1/2 cup (3 oz/90 g) fresh corn kernels

1 sprig fresh rosemary

3 sprigs fresh marjoram

5 sprigs fresh thyme

1/2 teaspoon salt

1/4 teaspoon freshly ground pepper

Put the saffron in a cup with the 1 tablespoon water and let stand for 10 minutes. Rinse the rice twice, drain, and set aside. In a medium saucepan, heat 2 tablespoons of the olive oil over medium heat, add the rice, saffron mixture, and turmeric. Stir for 1 minute. Add 2 1/4 cups (18 fl oz/560 ml) of the water and the salt, bring to boil over high heat, then reduce the heat to low, partially cover and simmer for 20 minutes, or until the rice is almost tender or slightly al dente.

In a small saucepan, bring the remaining 3/4 cup (6 fl oz/180 ml) water to a boil, add the peas, and reduce the heat to a simmer. Cook for 6 to 8 minutes, or until tender. Remove from the heat.

In a wok or large skillet, heat 3 tablespoons of the olive oil over medium heat and sauté the peppers for 2 minutes, or until slightly tender. Using a slotted spoon, transfer the peppers to a bowl. Add the zucchini to the pan and sauté for 2 minutes, or until slightly tender. Using a slotted spoon, transfer the zucchini to the same bowl with the peppers. Add another tablespoon of olive oil if needed, then add the onions, and sauté for 2 minutes, or until they start to soften. Add the tomatoes and simmer for 3 minutes, or until the liquid evaporates. Remove the peas from the pan with a slotted spoon and add the peas, corn, peppers, zucchini, rice, and fresh herbs to the wok. Simmer for 8 to 10 minutes over low heat or until rice is cooked, stirring occasionally to keep from sticking to the bottom of the pan. Remove the herb sprigs before serving.

<u>Variation</u>: One cup cooked chickpeas can be added along with with the final ingredients.

BUILD FAMILY
COOKING SKILLS

Black Bean Mushroom Patties

Makes 6 to 8 3-inch (7.5-cm) patties

Create your own veggie burgers, tailoring the ingredients to your taste. Pinto beans or other beans you prefer can offer a variation. The toasted coriander and cumin seeds add a robust flavor. Develop children's cooking skills by having them make the patties.

1 1/2 cups (10 1/2 oz/330 g) cooked black beans

2 tablespoons sesame oil

1/3 cup (1 1/2 oz/45 g) chopped yellow onion

1/3 cup (1 oz/30 g) chopped mushrooms

1 1/2 teaspoons coriander seeds, toasted and ground (page 221)

3/4 teaspoon cumin seeds, toasted and ground (page 221)

3/4 teaspoon salt

1 tablespoon organic psyllium husks

Put the beans in a medium bowl. In a medium skillet, heat 1 tablespoon of the oil over medium heat and sauté the onion and mushrooms for 1 or 2 minutes, or until they begin to soften. Add the coriander and cumin and sauté for 1 minute. Pour into the beans, add the salt and psyllium husks, and stir well. Use the back of a spoon or potato masher to mash the beans to a thick consistency. Taste and adjust the seasoning. Cover and refrigerate for 30 minutes to 1 hour.

Stovetop Method: Remove the bean mixture from the refrigerator. Heat the remaining 1 tablespoon oil in a medium skillet over medium heat. Oil your hands to keep the mixture from sticking to your fingers and form into 3-inch (7.5-cm) patties about 1/2 inch (12 mm) thick. Drop each patty into the hot skillet as you make it. Cook for 3 to 4 minutes or until the underside is toasted, then turn and repeat to cook on the other side.

Oven Method: Preheat the oven to 400°F (200°C) and oil a baking sheet. Form the bean mixture into patties as in the master recipe and place on the prepared baking sheet about 1 1/2 inches apart. Bake for 20 to 25 minutes, or until toasty brown on the bottom. Turn and bake another 20 to 25 minutes to cook the other side.

Notes: The pan frying method is quicker but the oven method uses less oil. To substitute commercial beans for home-cooked ones, use drained and rinsed Eden Organic black beans. If you like, you can add a tablespoon or two of flour to the bean mixture to make it thicker for forming the patties. Green onions can be substituted for yellow onions in this recipe. The Honey-Dijon Mustard Dressing (page 202) makes a tasty sauce.

FLAVORFUL
FUSION

Sweet-n-Spicy Adzuki Beans — Serves 4

The cinnamon, cloves and cayenne combine with the cumin seeds to give these beans a warming quality. The undercurrent of sweetness from the beets and molasses complements the spices to give these beans a unique flavor. Serve with rice and vegetable sides.

1 cup (7 oz/220 g) dried adzuki beans

4 cups (32 fl oz/ 1 l) water

1/2 cup (2 oz/60 g) peeled and grated raw beets

2 bay leaves

1 1/2-inch (4 cm) piece cinnamon stick

8 cloves

1 strip kombu (optional)

2 tablespoons blackstrap molasses

1 tablespoon apple cider vinegar

1 tablespoon tamari sauce, or coco aminos

1 teaspoon salt

2 tablespoons sesame oil

1 teaspoon cumin seeds

1 teaspoon mustard seeds

1 large onion, chopped

1/2 teaspoon ground turmeric

1/16 teaspoon cayenne pepper

Pick over the beans to remove small stones and dirt particles. Rinse, soak overnight in water to cover by 2 inches (5 cm). Drain and rinse.

In a medium pot, combine the beans, water, beets, bay leaves, cinnamon stick, cloves, and kombu. Bring to a boil over high heat, then reduce heat to medium-low, and simmer uncovered for 30 to 40 minutes, stirring occasionally. As needed, add small amounts of water to keep the beans from burning on the bottom of the pan. When the beans are done, they should be tender and have absorbed most of the water.

In a small bowl, combine the molasses, vinegar, tamari, and salt. Stir to blend. Set aside.

In a small skillet, heat the oil over medium heat. Add the cumin seeds and mustard seeds and toast, stirring until the seeds pop. Add the onion and sauté for 1 to 2 minutes, or until translucent. Add the turmeric and cayenne and sauté for 1 to 2 minutes. Add 2 tablespoons of the cooked beans with some of their cooking liquid to the pan and mash with the back of a wooden spoon. Reduce the heat to low and simmer for 1 to 2 minutes.

Add the onion mixture to the pot of beans and stir in the molasses mixture. Simmer over low heat until the liquid evaporates, 5 to 10 minutes. The beans should have a thick consistency, similar to refried beans for serving. Taste and adjust the seasoning.

<u>Pressure Cooker Method</u>: Soak the beans overnight as in the main recipe. Put the beans in a 4-quart (4-l) pressure cooker. Add 3 cups (24 fl oz/720 ml) water, beets, bay leaves, cinnamon stick, cloves, and kombu. Close and lock the pressure cooker. Bring to full pressure, then turn the heat to low, and cook for 15 to 20 minutes, or until the beans are tender.

<u>Variation</u>: Kidney or black beans may be substituted for the adzuki beans in this recipe. Conventional cooking time for these beans will be 1 to 1 1/2 hours.

PLEASING
DIVERGENCE

Sautéed Sweet Potato, Kale & Walnuts over Brown Rice

Serves 2

The flavors and textures of these vegetables with the walnuts offer a pleasing contrast to this easy to make meal. The sweet potato, kale, and walnut mixture can serve as a side dish without the rice.

3/4 cup (7 oz/220 g) short-grain brown rice

1 1/2 cups (12 fl oz/375 ml) water

1/2 teaspoon salt

2 tablespoons olive oil or ghee (page 57)

1 medium orange-fleshed sweet potato, peeled and diced into 3/8-inch (1 cm) pieces

1 bunch of kale, stemmed and cut into 1/2-inch (12-mm) strips

1/4 cup (2 fl oz/60 ml) water

1/2 cup (2 oz/60 g) walnuts, broken into pieces and soaked overnight

1/4 teaspoon salt

Rinse the rice twice and drain. In a medium saucepan, combine the rice, water, and salt. Bring the water to a boil over high heat, reduce the heat to low, cover, and simmer for 35 to 40 minutes, or until the water is completely absorbed and the rice is tender.

In a large skillet, heat the oil over medium heat and sauté the sweet potato for 3 to 5 minutes. Stir in the kale and sauté for 3 minutes. Add water and cook for 5 more minutes or until the sweet potatoes are tender. Stir in the walnuts and cook for 1 to 2 minutes, just long enough to heat the walnuts. Add the salt and serve over the cooked rice.

Note: When sweet potatoes are organic, leave the skins on.

Spiralizer variation: Heat oil, add the kale and then sauté for 2 minutes or until the kale starts to soften. Then add the spiralized sweet potatoes and walnuts and sauté for 2 to 3 minutes or until the sweet potatoes are tender.

MAKE BEANS MORE DIGESTIBLE

COOKING METHOD

Presoak beans overnight covered by at least 2 inches (5 cm) of water. After soaking, rinse them thoroughly. Then add to a large pot, cover the beans by 2 inches (5 cm) of water, bring to a boil, and simmer for 3 to 4 minutes. Remove from heat and let stand for 1 to 4 hours. The longer the beans stand, the more digestible and less gas-forming they will be. Faster-cooking beans such as mung beans may need to sit for only an hour, while black beans and chickpeas are best soaked for 3 to 4 hours.

After soaking, drain and rinse the beans and clean the pot. Put the beans back in the pot and add fresh water to cover by 2 inches (5 cm). To cook, bring to a boil over high heat. Then reduce the heat and simmer the beans uncovered for 1 to 2 hours or until tender, but not mushy. Stir occasionally and remove the foam as it accumulates on the surface of the broth.

INGREDIENT OPTIONS

- Cooking beans with a dash of the Indian spice asafoetida (hing) or a piece of kombu (sea kelp) can reduce flatulence.
- Adding 1 dried chile, 1/8 to 1/4 teaspoon ground black pepper, cayenne pepper, or chile powder to the beans before cooking can also help reduce flatulence.
- Adding 1 or 2 teaspoons lemon or lime juice or rice vinegar just before beans are fully cooked can enhance flavor and digestibility.
- Adding 1 teaspoon raisins or organic sugar or maple syrup during cooking will enrich flavor.

RICHLY
GRATIFYING

Swiss Chard-Portobellos Topped with Goat Cheese

Serves 4

The red onions, greens, and hearty Portobellos offer an appetizing array of flavors and textures. Serve with one or two side dishes, such as Delicately Sweet Carrots (page 187) or Sweet Potatoes with Ghee (page 190) to make a complete meal.

4 Portobello mushrooms, stems and gills removed
1 1/2 tablespoons extra-virgin olive oil
1 small red onion, finely chopped
2 cloves garlic, crushed
8 cups (8 1/2 oz/240 g) chopped chard
1 teaspoon minced fresh thyme
1/4 teaspoon salt
Freshly ground black pepper to taste
4 ounces (125 gms) goat cheese, cut into thin slices
Sesame seeds (optional)

Preheat the oven to 350°F (180°C). Place mushrooms in an oiled baking dish, stem side up.

In a medium skillet, heat the oil over medium heat and sauté the onion for 2 minutes, or until translucent. Add the garlic and sauté for 1 minute, then add the greens and thyme and sauté for 2 minutes more. Add the salt and freshly ground black pepper. Taste mixture and adjust seasoning. Remove from the heat, sprinkle the cavities of the mushrooms with salt, and fill with the onion mixture. Top with dabs of goat cheese.

Bake for 20 minutes, then remove from the oven, top with sesame seeds, and return to the oven for 10 more minutes, or until the mushrooms soften.

<u>Vegan version</u>: Ground sesame seeds or ground sunflower seeds may be substituted for goat cheese.

BOOST
ANTIOXIDANT INTAKE

Brown Rice Pasta with Broccoli & Umeboshi Plums

Serves 4

Bright green broccoli and red umeboshi plums make this dish a visual delight, and the contrasting textures and tastes are a palate-pleasing hit. This recipe was adapted from one by Kimiko Barber, author of *The Chopsticks Diet*.

1/4 cup (2 fl oz/60 ml) extra-virgin olive oil

4 cloves garlic, peeled and halved

12 ounces (375 g) brown rice pasta

1 pound (500 g) broccoli, cut into bite-sized florets

4 large or 6 small umeboshi plums, pitted and finely chopped

1/2 cup (2 oz/65 g) raw sunflower seeds, toasted (page 221)

In a small skillet, heat the oil and garlic over low heat for 2 minutes to infuse the oil. Remove from the heat.

Drop the pasta into a large pot of salted boiling water and cook at a rolling boil, until the pasta is al dente. Refer to package directions for approximate cooking time.

Meanwhile, blanch the broccoli in salted boiling water for 2 minutes; drain. Remove the garlic from the olive oil and heat the oil over low heat for 1 minute.

Drain the pasta and return to the pot. Add the umeboshi plums and olive oil. Toss well. Serve in warmed pasta bowls, top with broccoli, and garnish each serving with 2 tablespoons toasted sunflower seeds.

Note: Umeboshi plums can be found at Asian markets, natural foods stores, and online. If they are unavailable, 2 tablespoons of umeboshi paste may be substituted.

VEGETABLE SIDES

A gold-mine of essential phytochemicals, vegetables are the **#1** super food. Vegetables are also high in fiber, low in calories, and an excellent source of antioxidants. For these reasons, nutritionists recommend including three varieties of vegetables at each meal.

	Page
Lemon-Mustard Trumpet Mushrooms with Fresh Herbs	178
Blanched Rainbow Chard With Pine Nuts	180
Baked Spinach Topped with Ground Pumpkin Seeds	181
Sautéed Zucchini & Spinach with Dill	182
Ghee-Braised Celery	183
Beets-n-Butternut Squash	184
Red Cabbage Sesame Seed Sauté	185
Baked Parsnips in Miso-Almond Butter Sauce	186
Delicately Sweet Carrots	187
Kale Confetti	188
Lemon-Butter Roasted Cauliflower	189
Sweet Potatoes with Ghee	190

MUSHROOM MAGIC
HERBAL MELODY

Lemon-Mustard Trumpet Mushrooms with Fresh Herbs

Serves 4

The fleshy trumpets absorb the tangy mustard and lemon marinade beautifully, giving them a succulent quality. While baking, the sage, oregano, and thyme fill the kitchen with an inviting aroma.

14 ounces (440 g) royal trumpet mushrooms, cut into lengthwise slices, 1/4 inch (6mm) thick

1/2 cup (4 fl oz/120 ml) olive oil

Juice of 1 lemon

2 teaspoons Dijon mustard

1 tablespoon minced fresh sage, or 1 teaspoon dried

1 tablespoon minced fresh oregano, or 1 teaspoon dried

1 tablespoon minced fresh thyme, or 1 teaspoon dried

Salt and freshly-ground black pepper to taste

Put the mushrooms in a 9-inch (23-cm) square baking dish. In a small bowl, whisk all the remaining ingredients together. Taste and adjust the seasonings, then pour the herb mixture over the mushrooms, and let stand for 30 to 60 minutes, stirring occasionally so the seasoning is evenly absorbed.

Preheat the oven to 350°F (180°C) about 15 minutes before mushrooms are ready to be baked. Cover the baking dish and bake for 15 minutes. Uncover and bake for 15 minutes more, or until the mushrooms soften.

Note: Crimini or domestic mushrooms may be substituted for royal trumpet mushrooms. The left-over marinade makes a tasty salad dressing as well as a light sauce for steamed vegetables. Store in a glass jar in the refrigerator for up to 7 days.

Variations: Fresh marjoram as well as finely chopped fresh rosemary and parsley are good additions to this herbal blend. Have fun experimenting with the various varieties of Asian mushrooms found at farmers markets.

HIGH-POTENCY
NUTRIENT BOOST

Blanched Rainbow Chard with Pine Nuts

Serves 4 to 6

These tasty dark greens offer high-potency phytochemicals. The lemon juice and olive oil add tanginess to the blanched chard without being overpowering. The pine nuts complement the chard's even texture by adding a touch of crunch.

2 bunches rainbow chard

2 tablespoons fresh lemon juice

2 tablespoons olive oil

1/4 teaspoon salt

3 tablespoons pine nuts

Cut the stems from the leaves and chop the stems and leaves separately. In a small bowl, whisk the lemon juice, oil, and salt together.

In a large pot of salted boiling water, cook the chard stems for 1 to 2 minutes, then add the leaves and cook for 1 minute. Pour into a sieve, drain well, and place in a large bowl. Pour the oil mixture over the chard and toss gently. Garnish with the pine nuts. Serve warm as a side or cold as a salad.

<u>Variations</u>: Kale may be substituted for chard, blanch for 3 to 4 minutes. Toasted sunflower seeds (page 221) may be substituted for the pine nuts.

AUTUMN
SPECTACULAR

Baked Spinach Topped with Ground Pumpkin Seeds

Serves 4

The ground pumpkin seeds sautéed in ghee make a buttery, crusty topping for the steamed spinach. This easy-to-make side is rich and flavorful.

2 pounds (1 kg) spinach, stemmed and thoroughly rinsed

1 1/4 cups (4 oz/125 g) pumpkin seeds

3 tablespoons ghee (page 57), butter, or olive oil

1/4 teaspoon salt

Preheat the oven to 350°F (180°C). Steam the spinach for about 2 minutes or blanch in boiling water for 1 minute and drain completely. Squeeze out the excess liquid and place the spinach in a baking dish.

In a blender, grind the pumpkin seeds to a coarse texture. In a dry medium skillet over medium heat, melt the ghee and cook the ground seeds, stirring constantly, for 2 minutes. Add salt and spread the mixture evenly over the spinach, pressing it in lightly. Bake for 20 to 30 minutes, or until the topping looks lightly toasted.

Note: To hold this dish together, 2 beaten eggs may be mixed with spinach before adding the topping.

Variations: This dish may be made with chard or beet greens. Sesame seeds, sunflower seeds, or a combination may be substituted for the pumpkin seeds.

SHADES OF GREEN
TO TREASURE

Sautéed Zucchini & Spinach with Dill

Serves 4

The texture of the sautéed zucchini combines well with the tender spinach leaves to make an appetizing side. The dill brightens the light color of the zucchini and adds fresh flavor with a grassy aroma.

1 tablespoon olive oil

2 large or 4 small zucchini, sliced into 1/4-inch (6-mm) rounds

1 1/2 teaspoons minced fresh dill, or 1/2 teaspoon dried

2 cups (4 oz/125 g) chopped fresh spinach

Salt to taste

In a large skillet, heat the oil over medium heat. Add the zucchini and sauté until golden on one side, then turn, and sprinkle with the dill. Sauté for about 1 minute, then add the spinach, and stir until it softens, 1 or 2 minutes. Add salt and serve.

Note: While dill and fennel fronds are similar in appearance, their flavors are distinctly different. The taste of fennel is similar to black licorice and is not a suitable substitute for dill in this recipe.

QUICK
AND EASY

Ghee-Braised Celery — Serves 4

Braising is a simple way to bring out the flavor of almost any vegetable. It works particularly well with celery because of its fibrous texture and high water content.

1 tablespoon ghee (page 57), or butter

6 stalks celery, leafy tops removed, cut into 1-inch (2.5 cm) pieces

1 cup (8 fl oz/250 ml) water or vegetable broth

Salt and freshly ground black pepper to taste

In medium saucepan, melt the ghee over medium heat and sauté the celery for 4 to 5 minutes, or until it begins to soften. Add the water, cover, reduce the heat to low, and simmer for 10 minutes or until the celery is tender.

SURPRISE
YOURSELF WITH RICH FLAVOR

Beets-n-Butternut Squash — Serves 4

The warmth of the spices, the tender texture of the squash, combined with the sweetness of the beets blend together to produce a gratifying, mouthwatering side.

- 1 teaspoon arrowroot
- 1/4 cup (2 fl oz/60 ml) water
- 2 tablespoons sesame oil
- 2 teaspoons cumin seeds
- 2 cups (8 oz/250 g) coarsely-chopped yellow onions
- 3 cloves garlic, minced
- Dash of cayenne pepper
- 1 1/2 cups (7 oz/220 g) diced beets
- 3 cups (18 oz/560 g) peeled, seeded and chopped butternut squash
- 1 1/4 cup (10 fl oz/312 ml) water
- 1 teaspoon salt

Combine arrowroot with water in a small cup or bowl and stir to combine. In a medium saucepan, heat the oil over medium heat, add the cumin seeds, and cook for about one minute or until seeds pop. Add the onions and sauté for 3 minutes, or until translucent. Add the garlic, cayenne, and stir for 1 minute. Add the beets, squash, water, and salt. Bring to a boil over high heat, then reduce the heat to medium-low, cover, and simmer for 20 minutes, or until the vegetables are tender. Uncover, stir in the arrowroot mixture, increase the heat to medium-high, and simmer for 7 to 10 minutes, or until most of the liquid has evaporated, stirring often. The consistency should be similar to a thick jelly or jam.

SOAR WITH
COLOR AND CRUNCH

Red Cabbage Sesame Seed Sauté

Serves 4

The citrusy peppery quality of the caraway seeds gives this side a unique flavor while the sesame seeds add crunch. This cabbage sauté is inspired by a recipe in *Ayurvedic Cooking for Self-Healing* by Usha Lad and Dr. Vasant Lad.

- 2 tablespoons olive oil or ghee (page 57)
- 1 teaspoon caraway seeds
- 1 teaspoon cumin seeds
- 1 teaspoon brown mustard seeds
- 1 tablespoon brown sesame seeds
- 1 tablespoon black sesame seeds
- Dash of asafoetida (optional)
- 1/2 teaspoon ground turmeric
- Dash of cayenne pepper
- 6 cups (18 oz/560 g) finely chopped red cabbage
- 1/2 teaspoon salt

In a large skillet or wok, heat the oil over medium-high heat. Add the seeds and optional asafoetida and sauté 1 to 2 minutes or until the seeds pop. Add the turmeric, cayenne, cabbage, and salt. Stir-fry for 2 minutes. Reduce the heat to low, cover, and cook until the cabbage is crisp-tender about 8 to 10 minutes. Taste and adjust the seasoning.

Variations: White cabbage may be substituted for red or a combination of red and white may be used. One cup shredded carrots may replace one cup of white cabbage for an additional variation. Sunflower seeds may be substituted for sesame seeds.

SAVORY BLISS
COMPLEMENTARY FLAVORS

Baked Parsnips in Miso-Almond Butter Sauce

Serves 4

The miso-almond butter combination makes a rich sauce that enhances the flavor and texture of the parsnips. This sauce can serve as a topping on baked potatoes and works well with a variety of roasted vegetables.

4 cups (20 oz/625 g) peeled and thinly sliced in rounds parsnips

Sauce

1/4 cup (2 fl oz/ 60 ml) miso

1/4 cup (2 1/2 oz/75 g) almond butter

1/2 cup (4 fl oz/120 ml) water

Preheat the oven to 350°F (180°C). Line a rimmed baking sheet with parchment paper for easy cleaning. Put the parsnips in a medium bowl. In a small bowl, stir the miso, almond butter, and water together until smooth and creamy. Pour the sauce over the parsnips and stir until well coated. Allow to stand at room temperature for 20 minutes. Put the mixture into the prepared baking sheet. Bake for 35 to 40 minutes or until the parsnips are tender when forked. Serve warm.

Variation: Turnips may be substituted for parsnips and are especially delicious. This sauce is also tasty with winter squash and with steamed greens.

INDULGE
YOUR TASTE BUDS

⓪

Delicately Sweet Carrots — Serves 4

This simple recipe glazes the carrots to bring out their natural sweetness. The contrast of the fresh parsley with the orange carrots makes this dish visually appealing. Children love them.

5 carrots cut into rounds 1/4 inch (6 mm) thick

1 tablespoon ghee (page 57) or butter

1 teaspoon organic sugar or maple syrup

1 tablespoon finely chopped fresh marjoram or 1 teaspoon dried

1/2 cup (3/4 oz /20 g) chopped fresh flat-leaf parsley

Salt to taste

Steam the carrots over 2 inches (5 cm) boiling water in a covered steamer for 5 to 7 minutes, or until tender al dente. Set aside. Reserve the steaming liquid for soup broth.

In a medium skillet, melt the ghee over medium heat and stir in the sugar, marjoram, parsley, and salt. Add the carrots and cook for 2 minutes, or until well glazed.

CELEBRATE
THE SENSES

Kale Confetti

Serves 4 to 5

The dark green kale, orange carrots, and red bell pepper make a colorful presentation on a dinner plate. A versatile, nutrient-dense side dish that can be used as a filling for omelets, tacos, and wraps, as well as served cold as a salad.

- 1 tablespoon tamari sauce
- 1 tablespoon apple cider vinegar
- 1/4 cup (2 fl oz/60 ml) water
- 2 tablespoons sesame or olive oil
- 2 teaspoons caraway or cumin seeds
- 1/2 cup (2 1/2 oz/75 g) finely diced carrots
- 3/4 cup (4 oz/125 g) finely diced red bell pepper
- 1 bunch kale, stemmed, finely chopped
- 1/8 teaspoon freshly ground black pepper
- Salt to taste

In a small bowl, whisk the tamari, vinegar, and water together. In a large skillet or wok, heat the oil over medium heat, add the caraway seeds, and cook until the seeds pop. Add the carrots and bell pepper, and sauté for 3 minutes, or until the vegetables start to soften. Stir in the kale and black pepper. Stir in the tamari mixture, reduce the heat to low, and simmer, stirring occasionally, for 8 to 10 minutes, or until most of the liquid has evaporated and the kale and vegetables are tender. If the liquid evaporates before the vegetables are cooked, add 1 or 2 teaspoons of water to keep the kale from burning. Taste, adjust the seasoning, and serve.

<u>Variations</u>: Swiss chard or collard greens may be substituted for the kale. Rice vinegar may be substituted for the apple cider vinegar. To add more crunch, stir in 2 tablespoons toasted sesame or sunflower seeds before serving.

DELECTABLE
GOODNESS

Lemon-Butter Roasted Cauliflower

Serves 4

If you love a buttery, smooth texture, you'll find this roasted cauliflower basted with lemon-butter a gourmet delight.

2 small or 1 large cauliflower, trimmed
3 tablespoons ghee (page 57), unsalted butter, or olive oil
2 tablespoons fresh lemon juice
1/4 teaspoon salt
1/8 teaspoon freshly ground black pepper
Dash of freshly grated nutmeg

Preheat the oven to 350°F (180°C). In a covered steamer with 2 inches (5 cm) boiling water, steam the cauliflower for 10 minutes, or until almost tender.

Meanwhile, in a small saucepan, melt the ghee over low heat. Remove from the heat and stir in the lemon juice, salt, pepper, and nutmeg. Set aside.

Transfer the cauliflower to a deep baking dish, baste with one-third of the ghee mixture, cover, and bake for 10 minutes. Then baste again with another third of the seasoned ghee, cover, and bake for 10 more minutes. Then remove the cover, baste with the remaining seasoned ghee, and bake for 10 more minutes uncovered until the cauliflower is tender when the tip of a small knife is inserted in the center.

Variations: For a vegan version, substitute extra-virgin olive oil for the ghee. Two cloves of crushed garlic may be added to the basting combination in place of nutmeg. If you're a mustard fan, add 1 teaspoon Dijon mustard to the basting sauce along with the garlic.

RICHLY
SATISFYING

Sweet Potatoes with Ghee   Serves 4

Ghee brings the sweet potatoes to life with richness. Serve with dark leafy greens such as Kale Confetti (page 188) for a pleasing contrast in color and texture.

2 large orange-fleshed sweet potatoes
3 teaspoons ghee (page 57)
Salt to taste

Preheat the oven to 375°F (190°C). Pierce the sweet potatoes all over with a fork. Rub each sweet potato with about 1/2 teaspoon ghee and place in an oiled baking dish on the upper rack of the oven. Bake for 40 to 50 minutes, or until the sweet potatoes are tender when pierced with a small knife.

Remove from the oven and cut each sweet potato lengthwise, spread it open, and spoon 1/2 teaspoon ghee over each half. Season with salt and serve.

Variations: Baked russet potatoes are also good with ghee. Finely chop some chives to mix with the ghee and enjoy a tasty alternative to sour cream. For a vegan version, substitute extra-virgin olive oil for the ghee.

DESSERTS

Making your own desserts can help you control your sugar intake and help you avoid artificial sweeteners, highly processed oils, and trans fats. The recipes in this section are made with natural sweeteners or require no sweetener at all. They are nutritious and easy to make.

	Page
Sugarless Apple Crumble	192
Almond-Cardamom Macaroons	194
Dreamy Avocado Cream	195
Sesame-Molasses Butter Cookies	196
Carrot-Cacao Mousse	198

CINNAMON, SPICE
AND EVERYTHING NICE

Sugarless Apple Crumble — Serves 4

Dried cherries and candied ginger replace the sugar in this take on an American favorite, apple crisp. Serve for dessert or afternoon tea with Mint Chai (page 100).

4 large Granny Smith apples, cored and cut into 1-inch (2.5 cm) chunks
1/4 cup (1 1/2 oz/45 g) dried cherries
1/2 teaspoon ground cinnamon, plus more for dusting
2 whole cloves, crushed in a mortar and pestle
1/3 cup (3 fl oz/80 ml) water, plus more as needed

Topping
1/2 cup (1 1/2 oz/45 g) rolled (old-fashioned) oats
1/2 cup (2 1/2 oz/75 g) whole-wheat or spelt flour
1/8 teaspoon salt
2 tablespoons minced crystallized ginger, rinsed
1/4 cup (2 oz/60 g) ghee (page 57) or butter
1/4 cup (1 oz/30 g) chopped walnuts (optional)
2 to 4 tablespoons of water

Preheat the oven to 375°F (190°C). Oil a sided baking dish baking dish with ghee or butter.

In a small saucepan, combine the apples, cherries, cinnamon, and the cloves. Add the 1/3 cup (3 fl oz/80 ml) water and bring to a simmer. Remove from the heat, cover, and set aside.

In a medium bowl, combine the oats, flour, salt, and candied ginger and stir to blend. Cut in the ghee with a pastry blender or 2 dinner knives until the mixture is about the size of peas. Add the water and walnuts, if including. Mix lightly with a fork to just moisten the dough.

Using a slotted spoon, transfer the apple mixture to the prepared baking dish and reserve the cooking liquid. Cover the apples with the topping and bake in the center of the oven for 20 minutes. Remove from the oven and spoon 2 tablespoons of the cooking liquid from the apples over the topping. Dust with cinnamon and return to the oven for 10 minutes, or until the topping is golden and crusty. Remove from the oven and let cool for 10 minutes. Serve warm or at room temperature.

<u>Variations</u>: Pears, berries, or other seasonal fruit may be used in place of or in combination with the apples. For an added dimension of flavor in the crumble, try freshly grated nutmeg, ground cardamom, and ground allspice. Raisins or chopped dates can be substituted for the dried cherries.

CHEWY
COMPLEX FLAVOR

Almond-Cardamom Macaroons

Makes 12 to 15 cookies

These gluten-free cookies are crisp on the outside and gooey on the inside. For ultimate freshness make your own almond meal in a blender.

1 cup (3 1/2 oz/110 g) almond meal (page 219)

1/2 cup (2 oz/60 g) unsweetened finely shredded coconut

1/2 teaspoon freshly ground cardamom (about 7 to 8 pods)

1/8 teaspoon salt

1/4 cup (2 fl oz/60 ml) maple syrup

Preheat the oven to 325°F (170°C). Line a baking sheet with parchment paper.

In a medium bowl, combine all the ingredients and stir until blended. Form the mixture into balls the size of walnuts and place them 1 inch (2.5 cm) apart on the prepared pan. Bake for 12 to 15 minutes, or until tops are lightly golden. Remove from the oven and let cool on a wire rack. Store in an airtight container for up to 7 days.

Variation: Cashew grounds may be substituted for almond meal for an alternative taste and texture.

HEAVENLY
SWEETNESS

Dreamy Avocado Cream   Serves 4

The colorful tropical fruit smoothies sold at juice stands in Rio de Janeiro were the inspiration for this easy-to-make pudding. In Brazil, avocados are eaten as fruit, often with sugar added.

2 large or 3 medium avocados, pitted and peeled

1/3 cup (3 fl oz/80 ml) maple syrup or 1 tablespoon maple syrup and 2 tablespoons water with 5 to 6 drops stevia

Dash of salt

2 teaspoons fresh lime juice

8 tablespoons (4 fl oz/125 ml) water, as needed

Lime wedges for serving

In a blender, combine avocados, maple syrup, salt, and lime juice. Blend until smooth and creamy. Add water a tablespoon at a time as needed to make a thick mousse, stopping the blender to scrape down the sides as needed. Push through a sieve into a bowl to insure a smooth consistency. Serve with lime wedges alongside.

POWER PUNCH
SEED TREAT

Sesame-Molasses Butter Cookies

Makes 2 dozen squares

The almond butter adds richness and softens the molasses flavor to give these cookies an inviting taste. Sesame seeds are high in calcium, while molasses offers a potent source of iron.

1 3/4 cup (9 1/2 oz/275 g) rice or spelt flour

1/2 cup (2 1/2 oz/70 g) sesame seeds

1/4 teaspoon salt

3/4 cups plus 2 tablespoons ghee (page 57), or softened butter

1/4 cup (2 fl oz/60 g) molasses

1/4 cup (2 1/2 oz/75 g) almond butter

In a medium bowl, combine the flour, sesame seeds, and salt. Stir with a whisk to blend. In a large bowl, combine the ghee, molasses, and almond butter and stir until smooth. Add the dry ingredients to the molasses mixture and stir to make dough. Refrigerate for 30 to 45 minutes or until dough is stiff enough to form into logs. Remove from the refrigerator.

Transfer to a cutting board and form into 2 logs, each about 7 inches (18 cm) long and 1 1/2 inches (4 cm) in diameter. Wrap in wax paper and refrigerate for 40 to 60 minutes or until logs are firm.

Preheat the oven to 350°F (180°C) 15 to 20 minutes before removing logs from the refrigerator. Remove the dough from the refrigerator and cut into slices 3/8 inch (1 cm) thick. Place on baking sheet and bake for 12 to 15 minutes. When the cookies are done they will offer a slight resistance when lightly pressed. If they yield easily, then they need more time. If they brown around the edges they are overdone. Let cool on the baking sheet for 10 minutes, then use a metal spatula to transfer to a wire rack. Let cool completely.

Variations: For a tasty alternative, combine 1/4 cup (1 1/4 oz/35 g) sunflower seeds and 1/4 cup (1 1/4 oz/35 g) sesame seeds. Also, try substituting finely chopped almonds or walnuts for the sesame seeds.

SIN-FREE
INDULGENCE

Carrot-Cacao Mousse

Serves 4

The natural sweetness of carrots makes them ideal for a sugar-free dessert. This nutritious treat is also dairy-free.

---

1 1/2 pounds (675 g) carrots, cut into 1/4 inch (6 mm) rounds

1/4 teaspoon salt

1/4 cup (3/4 oz/20 g) unsweetened cocoa powder

1 teaspoon vanilla extract

2 tablespoons raw honey

1 teaspoon ghee (page 57) or butter (optional)

Put the carrots in a medium saucepan and add water to cover. Bring to a boil, then reduce the heat to medium, cover, and cook until nicely tender when forked, about 12 to 15 minutes. Remove from the heat and let cool slightly. Using a slotted spoon, transfer the carrots to a blender with 1/4 cup (2 fl oz/60 ml) of the cooking liquid. Add all the remaining ingredients and purée until smooth. To guarantee a creamy consistency push through a sieve with a spatula or wooden spoon. Spoon into dessert goblets and refrigerate for 30 minutes or up to 2 hours before serving.

DRESSINGS SAUCES CONDIMENTS

Dressings and sauces can be made in advance, then at mealtimes spooned over salads, cooked vegetables, pastas, and grains. Highlight to a meal and aid digestion with condiments. Keep a jar or two in the refrigerator so you can put a meal together quickly when you are short on time.

	Page
Dressings & Sauces	201
Condiments	209

DRESSINGS & SAUCES

Reduce the risk of consuming unhealthful food additives by making your own dressings. Store-bought dressings are often high in calories and may contain processed oils, trans fats, and artificial sweeteners.

	Page
Honey-Dijon Mustard Dressing	202
Umeboshi Plum Dressing	203
Oil-Free Lemon-Ginger Dressing	204
Sunflower-Dill Dressing	205
Pistachio Pesto Sauce	206
Tomato Sauce For All Occasions	207

DRESS UP
YOUR SALAD

Honey-Dijon Mustard Dressing

Makes 3/4 cup (6 fl oz/180 ml)

The tangy sweetness of this dressing goes well with fresh greens that are slightly peppery, like arugula. This recipe was given to me by Ann Snyder of Snyder Honey.

2 tablespoons Dijon mustard
2 tablespoons raw honey
1/4 cup (2 fl oz/60 ml) apple cider vinegar
1/3 cup (3 fl oz/80 ml) extra-virgin olive oil
Salt and freshly ground black pepper to taste

In a small bowl, whisk the mustard and honey together until smooth. Whisk in the vinegar to blend. Whisk in the olive oil a tablespoonful at a time until smooth. Season with salt and pepper. Store in a closed jar in the refrigerator for up to 7 days.

Note: Juice from one lemon may be substituted for the apple cider vinegar. This dressing may also be made in a blender.

MAXIMIZE
ANTIOXIDANT INTAKE

Umeboshi Plum Dressing

Makes 2/3 cup (5 fl oz/160 ml)

This 3-ingredient dressing adds a tangy zing to salads of fresh, mixed greens.

---

4 umeboshi plums, pitted and chopped

3 tablespoons apple cider vinegar

1/2 cup (4 fl oz/125 ml) avocado oil

In a small bowl, mash the plums with a pestle. Whisk the vinegar and oil until well blended and add the umeboshi. This can be made in a blender or by shaking the ingredients together in a closed jar. When serving, spoon from the bottom of the jar as the umeboshi plums tend to settle at the bottom. Store in a closed glass container in the refrigerator for up to 7 days.

Note: Rice vinegar can substitute for apple cider vinegar and 2 to 3 teaspoons of umeboshi paste can be substituted for plums. Umeboshi plums and paste can be found in Asian markets, some natural food stores, and on-line.

KINDLE
DIGESTIVE FIRE

Oil-Free Lemon-Ginger Dressing

Makes 1/2 cup (4 fl oz/125 ml)

This Asian style dressing adds a gentle sweetness to mild greens, such as butter lettuce or mâche. Serve as a starter to stimulate digestive juices.

2 tablespoons tamari sauce or coco aminos

2 tablespoons raw honey

2 tablespoons fresh lemon juice

1/4 cup (2 fl oz/60 ml) water

2 teaspoons finely grated peeled ginger

Combine all the ingredients in a blender or whisk together in a small bowl until smooth. Store in a closed glass jar in the refrigerator for up to 7 days. Shake the jar of dressing before pouring over salad greens as the ginger tends to settle at the bottom.

ADD
SOME RICHNESS

Sunflower-Dill Dressing

Makes 2/3 cup (5 fl oz/160 ml)

This creamy dairy-free dressing is perfect for salad lovers that prefer a thicker dressing. Try it spooned over steamed vegetables for added flavor.

1/4 cup (1 oz/30 g) sunflower seeds

1/4 cup (2 fl oz/60 ml) water

1 1/2 teaspoons finely chopped fresh dill, or 1/2 teaspoon dried

2 teaspoons fresh lemon juice

2 teaspoons raw honey

1/4 cup (2 fl oz/60 ml) extra-virgin olive oil

1/8 teaspoon salt

In a blender or small food processor, grind the seeds to a powder. Add all the remaining ingredients and blend until smooth. Store in a closed glass jar in the refrigerator for up to 7 days.

Note: Pumpkin or hemp seeds may used in place of the sunflower seeds. If the consistency is too thick, add 2 to 4 tablespoons of water and blend.

HIT THE
HIGH NOTES

Pistachio Pesto

Makes 3/4 cup (6 fl oz/180 ml)

The toasted pistachios with fresh basil turn this classic pasta sauce a luscious deep green. The nutritional yeast replaces Parmesan cheese to create buttery richness.

1/2 cup (2 oz/60 g) shelled pistachios
1 bunch fresh basil, stemmed and coarsely chopped
1/4 cup (1/2 oz/15 g) minced fresh flat-leaf parsley or fresh cilantro
2 cloves garlic, minced
Dash each of salt and freshly ground black pepper
1/2 cup (4 fl oz/125 ml) extra-virgin olive oil
2 tablespoons nutritional yeast

In a dry medium skillet, stir the pistachios over medium heat until fragrant and lightly toasted. Empty nuts into a blender and chop finely, but not to a powder. Add basil, parsley, garlic, salt, pepper, and olive oil to the pistachios and purée, stopping the blender to push the leaves down as needed until a smooth consistency is achieved. Blend in the nutritional yeast.

Serve over your favorite whole-grain pasta, such as brown rice rotini, or steamed vegetables. The pesto is also good to spread on toast and on bread for sandwiches.

Note: To mix the pesto with the pasta easily, dilute the pesto sauce with a tablespoon or two of the cooking water from the pasta just before serving. This warms the sauce and helps it combine evenly with the pasta.

Variations: Walnuts or pine nuts may be substituted for the pistachios. Parmesan or pecorino cheese can be used for a non-vegan pesto in place of the nutritional yeast.

DELIGHT
LOVED ONES

Tomato Sauce For All Occasions

Makes 2 1/2 cups (20 fl oz/625 ml)

This flavorful sauce is perfect for eggplant parmesan, lasagna, Spanish rice, and stuffed bell peppers. The carrots accentuate the sweetness of the tomatoes, add flavor and soften the pungency of the cayenne.

3 tablespoons olive oil

1 cup (5 oz/155 g) finely chopped yellow onion

1/2 cup (2 1/2 oz/75 g) finely chopped carrot

1 teaspoon dried oregano

1 1/2 teaspoons minced fresh thyme, or 1/2 teaspoon dried

1 1/2 teaspoons minced fresh basil, or 1/2 teaspoon dried

1/4 teaspoon herbes de Provence

Dash of cayenne pepper

2 pounds (1 kg) tomatoes, peeled, seeded, and chopped (pages 220-221)

Water as needed

1/2 to 1 teaspoon salt

In a large saucepan, heat the oil over medium heat and sauté the onion for 2 minutes, or until translucent. Stir in the carrot, herbs, and cayenne and sauté for 2 minutes. Add the tomatoes, bring to a boil, reduce the heat to medium-low, and simmer for 40 minutes to 1 hour, stirring occasionally until flavorful and desired consistency is attained. If the sauce becomes too thick, add water in small amounts. Season with salt and freshly ground pepper to taste.

CONDIMENTS

Liven up any meal with one of the condiment recipes in this section. In Ayurvedic and Indian cuisine condiments serve to stimulate the palate and aid digestion. A tablespoon or two of a condiment on a plate can add visual appeal, plus complementary flavors and textures.

	Page
Coconut-Cucumber-Cilantro Raita	210
Date-Mint Chutney	211
Parsley-Mint Chutney	212
Oven-Roasted Tomatoes with Fresh Herbs	213

DELICIOUS
DIVERSION

Coconut-Cucumber-Cilantro Raita

Makes 1 1/2 cups (12 oz/375 g)

The cooling effect of this traditional condiment can serve to balance spicy dishes. In warm weather months it can be served to refresh and rejuvenate body, mind, and spirit.

1 cup (8 oz/250 g) plain organic whole milk yogurt

1 cup chopped cucumbers, peeled and seeds removed

1/2 cup (2 oz/60 g) unsweetened grated coconut, lightly toasted

1/2 cup (1/2 oz/15 g) fresh cilantro leaves, chopped

1 teaspoon maple syrup or raw honey or 1 teaspoon water with 2 drops stevia

1/4 teaspoon salt

Spoon the yogurt into a medium bowl and stir in all the remaining ingredients. Store in a closed glass jar in the refrigerator for up to 5 days.

Vegan Option: Coconut, oat, or cashew yogurt may be substituted for dairy.

FEEL
LUSCIOUSLY ALIVE

Date-Mint Chutney

Makes 3/4 cup (9 oz/250 g)

The jalapeño chile, ginger, and garlic add a pungency that balances nicely with the sweet dates and refreshing mint. This condiment includes four of the five tastes: sweet, sour, salty, and pungent, making it a digestive aid according to Ayurveda.

10 to 12 Medjool dates, pitted and chopped

Leaves from 1 large bunch fresh mint, chopped

1 tablespoon minced garlic

1 teaspoon finely grated peeled ginger

1 teaspoon seeded and minced jalapeno chile

1/2 teaspoon salt

3 tablespoons fresh lemon juice

In a medium bowl, combine the dates and mint. In a mortar, combine the ginger, garlic, and chile, add the salt and crush to a paste with a pestle. Add the ginger mixture and lemon juice to the dates and mint, and mash with a fork or pulse in a mini food processor to a paste. To allow flavors to develop let stand at room temperature for at least 1 hour or up to 2 hours before serving. Store in a closed glass jar in refrigerator for up to 7 days.

ACCENTUATE
DINING PLEASURE

Parsley-Mint Chutney

Makes 1 cup (8 oz/250 g)

This condiment goes well with Sweet-n-Spicy Adzuki Beans (page 170) and Split Red Lentils & Basmati Rice (page 162). Spread on seeded crackers for a quick snack.

1 1/2 cups (1 1/2 oz/45 g) fresh flat-leaf parsley leaves

1 1/2 cups (1 1/2 oz/45 g) fresh mint leaves

1/4 cup (2 oz/60 ml) water, plus more as needed

Juice of 1 lime

1/2 cup (2 oz/60 g) unsweetened shredded coconut

1 inch (2 cm) fresh ginger, peeled and finely chopped

1 teaspoon raw honey

1/2 teaspoon sea salt

1/4 teaspoon freshly ground pepper

In a blender or a small food processor, combine the parsley, mint, water, and lime juice and blend to a purée. Add all the remaining ingredients and blend to a smooth paste. A tablespoonful of water may be added as needed to achieve a smooth paste. Store in a sealed glass jar in the refrigerator for up to 5 days.

Variations: Cilantro may be substituted for the parsley or the mint and rice syrup or maple syrup for the honey. Parsley and cilantro combo offer a tasty, health benefitting alternative.

DAZZLE
THE DINNER PLATE

Oven-Roasted Tomatoes with Fresh Herbs

Makes 1 cup (8 oz/250 g)

These tomatoes make a colorful, sweet and tangy condiment that can add a unique taste to green salads. The moist carmelized Early Girl tomatoes make a tantelizing garnish on pasta served with Pistachio Pesto. (page 206)

12 ounces (375 g) small Early Girl tomatoes or one basket cherry tomatoes

Salt to taste.

1 1/2 teaspoons minced fresh marjoram, or 1/2 teaspoon dried

1 1/2 teaspoons minced fresh thyme, or 1/2 teaspoon dried

1 1/2 teaspoons minced fresh basil, or 1/2 teaspoon dried

3 tablespoons extra-virgin olive oil

Preheat the oven to 375°F (180°C). Cut the tomatoes in half and place cut side up fitting them tightly together in the bottom of a sided baking dish. The tomatoes should fill the bottom of the dish and fit together tightly without overlapping. Dust with salt. In a small bowl, mix the herbs together and sprinkle evenly over the tomatoes. Then drizzle with the olive oil.

Bake for 30 to 45 minutes, or until the tomatoes start to shrink. Check the tomatoes after 30 minutes and watch them closely near the end of cooking time to keep them from burning. Remove from the oven. Serve hot or at room temperature.

Note: The olive oil and herbs may be mixed the night before to infuse the flavors. Double the recipe to serve 4 as a side dish.

INTERVIEW

Raw Honey: A Mystical Universe

Bill Snyder, Snyder Honey

Throughout history honey has been valued as a curative. In 400 B.C. to prepare for Olympic games, Greek athletes consumed honey to raise their energy level. Ancient Romans took a glass of water with honey and vinegar to cleanse their system. Egyptians applied honey on wounds for healing, and Mohammad referred to it as a "remedy for every illness."

At the farmers market at Ferry Plaza in San Francisco, I was pleased to meet Bill Snyder, the second-generation beekeeper of Snyder Honey. He had a wide range of products displayed and that prompted me to ask him questions about honey production.

Bill has been around bees all his life. When he was a child, his father started keeping bees as a hobby. As a teenager, Bill helped his father care for the hives. Over time, the bee keeping grew into a family business that Bill expanded by adding products such as bee pollen, propolis, lip balm, and beeswax candles.

Honey and honey production are more than taking honey from the hives or a natural sweetener to spread on bread, Bill told me. Honey production involves subtle elements of nature, such as sunlight, flowers, and the freshness of springtime.

Why did you become a beekeeper?

Working with bees is rewarding. It is productive, vigorous work that keeps me physically fit. I like it because I'm always learning.

Could you say more about that?

There is more to honey production than extracting it from the hives. Honey is a product of nature, and nature is constantly changing. No two seasons are ever the same, and each hive has its own unique character. Keeping bees is challenging and exciting because you must always be alert and ready to adapt to changing conditions.

What do you like most about beekeeping?

Always having pure honey and bee products for my family is one. Another is providing quality bee products for customers who like honey's sweet taste and healthful properties. Most of all, it is working with the bees. They keep me connected to the seasons and the flow of nature. When the bees are building up in the spring, I can really feel the pulse of life.

I've read that raw honey can sooth a sore throat, quiet a cough, and heal wounds. Have you ever used it to cure anything?

When I was fifteen, I was running down some stairs barefoot. I slid and tore all the skin off the sole of my right foot. I immediately smothered it with raw honey, and in five or six days it healed.

That is remarkable. Tell me about beekeeping and honey production. Where does honey come from and what does it consist of?

Bees convert the nectar that comes from flowers to honey. It is about 80 percent moisture combined with complex sugars. Honey is one of the purest, most natural foods.

How do bees make honey?

Honeybees collect nectar from the flowers of clover, fruit trees, and berry bushes by sucking it out with their tube-like tongues. They store it in their "honey stomachs". When they return to the hive, the worker bees take the nectar from the honeybees. The worker bees then chew the nectar to break down the complex sugars into simple ones, which prevents the substance from being attacked by bacteria.

Next, the bees fill the cells of the honeycomb with this nectar and fan it with their wings to evaporate the moisture, leaving a thick, syrupy liquid. When the cells are full, worker bees seal them with wax, where the honey remains stored until needed.

How do the seasons influence honey production?

It depends on the location. In California, the bees begin collecting nectar in mid-February with spring almond blossoms, and hives can grow to five times their size within several weeks. There may be a surplus of honey by May, and then harvesting it can begin. But there is no set time or way. The production of honey depends on the rhythms of nature.

Are there other vital factors that influence beekeeping?

There is a saying among beekeepers that the location is more important than the bees. Every location has a different microclimate, which has a strong influence on every aspect of honey production.

Do the hives require attention all year round?

Absolutely. Keeping hives productive requires constant attention.

How can consumers identify a high-quality honey?

Get to know the vendors and ask them questions. Then follow your instincts based on what you learn. Also, look at how the honey is packaged. A quality product is generally stored in glass. Honey is so pure that it does not require heating or much processing. In fact, pasteurization results in lower quality honey, as the heat involved will diminish its nutritional value and anti-bacterial attributes. Honey with a cloudy appearance can indicate minimal processing. Look for raw honey or honey in a comb for the highest quality.

When honey crystallizes does that mean it has spoiled?

No. Crystallization is a natural process that happens with time. To bring crystallized honey back to syrup, place the entire jar in water that has been heated to about 90°F (32°C) for 15 to 20 minutes.

How long does honey keep, and what is the best way to store it?

Raw honey is so pure that when stored properly, it lasts indefinitely. However, the presence of moisture can cause honey to ferment and spoil, so it's best to store honey in a sealed glass jar in a cool dark place. To avoid contamination, always use a clean, dry spoon or knife when dipping into the honey jar.

There are many varieties of honey. Are some more nutritious than others?

Every drop of honey is a treasure chest of minerals, vitamins, amino acids, and enzymes. The exact combination depends on the nectars it comes from. Oak and avocado nectars produce a darker, stronger-flavored honey that is said to be highest in minerals.

Bill and his wife, Ann, are conscientious about environmental issues and their operation produces little to no waste products. They work hard to deliver a high-quality product to their customers.

Learn more at:
http://www.snydershoney.com

Love and Support Pollinators

Whether you keep a small flower box on a balcony or a windowsill in the city or cultivate a garden in your yard, here are practical steps you can take to sustain the health, abundance, and diversity of bees, butterflies, and other pollinators.

Create a Diversity of Bloom

Bees and butterflies need access to plentiful sources of nectar and pollen throughout the growing season. Fill your garden with native flowers and heritage plant varieties that enable bees and beneficial insects to flourish. Cultivate diverse flower colors, shapes, and bloom times. Start with three species of flowers in bloom each season to create an environment of year-round, uninterrupted bloom, which is ideal for colony reproduction. Pollen is essential nutrition for bee larva. Avoid growing flowers with double petals and varieties that produce no pollen because they offer little benefit.

Protect Nests and Egg-Laying Sites

Native bees are the most important group of pollinators. Help them to flourish by setting up some areas in your garden for them to nest and lay eggs. Favorite nesting habitats include: open sandy ground (sweat bees, long-horned bees), brush piles (bumblebees), and old tree stumps (mason bees, leafcutter bees). Supplemental nesting for these precious pollinators can be created with bee blocks or bundles of hollow plant stems.

Refrain From Using Pesticides

Most lawn and garden problems can be resolved without the use of pesticides. Note that even "organic-approved" products can harm pollinators and other wildlife. Although herbicides are usually not directly lethal to insects, they can reduce plant diversity and diminish the noninvasive wildflowers that provide essential pollen and nectar for butterflies, hummingbirds, and bees. Learn more at

www.xerces.org and www.BringBackthePollinators.org.

How-To Basics

These basic techniques are used throughout the cookbook and are explained here to assist you when making the recipes.

Making Almond Meal

Almond meal is finely ground raw almonds. Homemade meal will always be fresher than any store bought variety. Grind raw almonds 1/2 cup (2 1/2 oz/75 g) at a time in a blender or mini food processor until fine. Almonds may be skinned or blanched as described below before grinding into meal.

Making Almond Milk

Soak 1/2 cup (2 oz/60 g) raw almonds overnight in purified water. In the morning rinse the almonds. Add to blender along with 2 cups (16 fl oz/500 ml) purified water. Blend until the almonds are crushed and the liquid is creamy. Stop the blender once or twice and with a chop stick dislodge any almonds that may be stuck under the blades. Pour the mixture into a nylon nut milk bag. Tighten the draw string on the milk bag and slowly squeeze the milk out into a bowl. Store in a glass jar in the refrigerator for up to 3 days. Nylon milk bags can be found in natural food stores and online.   Makes 2 cups (16 fl oz/500 ml)

Blanching Almonds

To blanch almonds, put raw almonds in a bowl, pour boiled water over them, and let stand for 1 to 2 minutes. Drain and run cold water over the almonds. Pinch the almonds to pop them easily out of their skins.

Making Coconut Milk

Bring 2 cups (16 fl oz/500 ml) water to a boil. Add 1/2 cup (2 oz/60 g) unsweetened, grated coconut and remove from heat. Allow to cool for 5 to 10 minutes. Pour into a blender, and start the blender on a low speed. Then gradually turn to a medium-high speed. Let stand for 10 minutes to cool, then pour into a nylon milk bag, tighten the drawstring on the milk bag and slowly squeeze out the milk into a bowl. Use immediately or store in a sealed glass jar in the refrigerator for up to 3 days.

Grinding Chia, Flax, and Hemp Seeds

Grind seeds in a coffee grinder and store in an airtight container in the refrigerator. Grinding enhances absorbability. The oils that seeds contain are fragile, so grind them in small quantities and use within ten days. Sprinkle 1 to 3 teaspoons on cereals, salads, soups, and veggies.

Grinding Herbs and Spices

To get the most flavor from herbs and spices, grind them just before using. Use a coffee grinder, spice grinder, mortar and pestle, or mini food processor.

Peeling Tomatoes

Make a crosswise cut on the bottom of each tomato, then drop into boiling water for 1 or 2 minutes. Using a slotted spoon, transfer to a bowl of ice water for a few seconds. Remove and allow to cool. The skins can then be easly peeled away.

Pickling Ginger

Peel and cut a 1 1/2-inch (4 cm) piece of fresh ginger into thin slivers about 1/2-inch (2 mm) long. Add the juice of 1 freshly squeezed lemon or lime and add 1/8 teaspoon salt. Pour the mixture into a small glass jar, cover, and marinate in the refrigerator for 12 hours. Store for up to 7 days. To stimulate digestion, chew 2 or 3 pieces of the marinated ginger 15 to 20 minutes before your meal.

Seeding Tomatoes

Cut the tomatoes in half crosswise and hold cut side down over the sink, squeeze slightly and shake to remove the seeds.

Toasting Nuts and Seeds

<u>Oven method</u>: Spread nuts or seeds evenly on a rimmed baking sheet or in a pie tin and bake in a preheated 300°F (150°C) oven for 5 to 10 minutes, or until you sense a toasted aroma.

<u>Pan method</u>: Put the nuts or seeds in a dry skillet over medium heat and stir until they become golden. You may sense a toasted aroma. Take care not to let them burn. When toasted, transfer to a pie pan or bowl to stop the cooking. Allow them to cool completely. Eat as a snack or use as a garnish on salads or over rice, pasta, or sautéed vegetables.

Toasting Spices

When whole spices are toasted they release their oils which amplifies their natural flavor. Heat a small skillet without oil over medium heat. Add the spices and stir until fragrant. Spices toast quickly, so pay close attention to prevent them from burning.

Ingredient Glossary

Apple cider vinegar: Antibacterial, antiviral, and antifungal, this vinegar promotes a healthy immune system and pH balance in the blood. It is rich in enzymes and potassium and adds a zestiness to food. I use Bragg's Raw Apple Cider Vinegar, which is unfiltered, unheated, and unpasteurized.

Amaranth: See Gluten-Free Whole Grains, page 47.

Asafoetida or hing: This dried gum resin comes from the ferula plant and is quite pungent, so no more than 1/16 teaspoon should be used in recipes serving 4 to 6. This spice is a digestive that reduces the gaseous effects of legumes and cruciferous vegetables such as cabbage. A dash of asafoetida can be dropped into hot oil and allowed to fry for a second or two before adding other ingredients. Available in Indian groceries, organic food stores, and online.

Barley: Barley has been used in many countries for centuries. It is a cereal grain with a chewy texture and mild nutty flavor. Barley is available in pearl and hulled forms. Pearl barley is not a whole grain because much of the outer bran layer has been removed. The hulled form is more nutritious as the bran is left intact. Both types of barley are low on the glycemic index.

Basil: Native to India, basil was introduced to Europe in the eighteenth century. Among its more than forty varieties, the best known are the sweet, red, and Thai basil. With a strong, sweet aroma, basil is pungent and heating. Select fresh basil with shiny, bright leaves without dark spots. Use the leaves and discard the stems. Basil darkens when bruised or added to anything hot, so add near the end of the cooking process.

Bay leaves (sweet laurel): Aromatic, sweet, and pungent, bay leaves can aid digestion and minimize the gaseous effects of beans and legumes. Remove the leaves before serving.

Black peppercorns: These are berries that have been harvested unripe and sun-dried. For the fullest flavor, grind peppercorns immediately before use, as aromatic characteristics of pepper evaporate quickly once ground. The finer the grind, the less bite the pepper will have, as its oils become more dispersed.

Brown rice: See Gluten-Free Whole Grains, page 47.

Brown rice syrup: Moderately sweet with a butterscotch flavor, this syrup is a good replacement for less healthy sweeteners in baking. In a recipe calling for 1 cup (8 oz/250 g) of white sugar, substitute 1/4 cup (2 fl oz/60 ml) brown rice syrup and reduce the other liquid ingredients in the recipe by 1/4 cup (2 fl oz/60 ml).

Buckwheat: See Gluten-Free Whole Grains, page 47.

Cardamom: Native to India and Indonesia this spice has a complex flavor profile and is highly aromatic. It is most often used in sweets, beverages, and Indian-inspired dishes. Cardamom can be purchased as pods, seeds, or powder. When only a small amount of ground cardamom is needed, grind the seeds with a mortar and pestle for maximum flavor. Cardamom is available in green, white, or black pods, all containing small black seeds. Green cardamom, the most common variety, is often used in sweeter dishes but works in savory dishes as well. The white pods are green pods that have been bleached, resulting in a more faded flavor and aroma. Black cardamom pods have a smoky flavor and are most often found in savory dishes.

Cayenne: This potent spice ground from sun-dried, red-hot cayenne chiles can be substituted for green chiles in Indian recipes. A dash or two adds mild heat, while 1/8 teaspoon or more will make a dish that serves four quite piquant. Cayenne is used in Ayurvedic cooking to kindle digestive fire and to reduce phlegm and inflammation.

Cilantro (fresh coriander): This leafy green herb grows abundantly in South America and tropical climates and is one of India's favorite herbs. It is used to flavor food and as a garnish. Use only the leaves; the stems can be saved to make soup broth.

Cinnamon: See Medicinal Spices, page 63.

Cloves: See Medicinal Spices, page 64.

Coco Aminos: See Tamari page 232.

Coconut oil: Made from a pressing of coconut meat, this oil is solid at room temperature and melts to a liquid when heated. Stable in cooking and baking, coconut oil can replace dairy for people who are lactose-intolerant and for those on vegan diets. There are two main forms of coconut oil, virgin and refined: Virgin coconut oil contains high amounts of vitamin E and polyphenols that offer antioxidant properties. The virgin form can impart a strong coconut flavor, while the refined has a milder taste. For health purposes coconut oil can be used to eliminate toxins as in oil pulling (page 18). Due to its high level of saturated fat, it is recommended to consume in moderation.

Coconut palm sugar: Reminiscent of brown sugar, this grainy, sweet powder is composed of sucrose and fructose and contains some fiber, potassium, magnesium, zinc, iron, vitamins B1, B2, B3, B6, and amino acids. Made from the sap of the coconut palm and is minimally processed. This coconut sugar is the traditional sweetener of Southeast Asia. Read the label to insure that it's 100% coconut sugar, as the sugars from other varieties of palm do not have the same qualities.

Coriander seeds: See Medicinal Spices, page 64.

Cumin seeds: See Medicinal Spices, page 65.

Dill: The feathery fresh leaves and the flower head contain vitamin C. Dill seeds help prevent indigestion, nausea, and heartburn. Dill is bitter, astringent, pungent, and heating.

Fennel: See Medicinal Spices, page 66

Garlic: This popular, versatile herb has a distinctive flavor that varies from pungent to sweet. To take advantage of garlic's antiviral and antibacterial properties, crush and let stand for 10 minutes before adding to food. This allows the compounds in the garlic to combine, increasing its preventive attributes. Garlic becomes sweeter and milder when cooked. Sauté it briefly over low to medium heat until fragrant and lightly golden. Be vigilant as it can burn easily.

Ginger: See Medicinal Spices, page 67.

Green onions (also called scallions): These are onions that are harvested before the bulbs mature. Green onions are suitable for foods that call for milder flavoring and are often added at the end of cooking (as in miso soup) or served finely chopped as a garnish on a dish. Both the green tops and the white bulbs may be used.

Honey: According to ancient Ayurvedic literature, honey should never be cooked. "If cooked, the molecules become a non-homogenized glue that adheres to mucus membranes and clogs subtle channels, producing toxins. Uncooked honey is nectar. Cooked honey is considered poison." (Lad: 47). See Raw Honey: A Mystical Universe, pages 214-217.

Horsetail: This ancient plant grows near water and is very high in silica. As a traditional herbal remedy, its potential benefits include promoting bone, teeth, nail, and hair health. Externally, it can be used as a compress to reduce inflammation and draw out infection from boils, and sores.

Kombu: This is a leafy kelp with a savory *umami* flavor. It is a good source of calcium, folate, and magnesium. Add it to beans and legumes during cooking to bring out flavor and to reduce flatulence. To make a vegetarian broth for soups and stews, add a 4- to 6-inch (10 to 15 cm) strip of kombu to 4 cups (32 fl oz/1 l) water. Cover and simmer for 15 to 20 minutes over low heat. The simmered kombu can be composted or cut into 1/4-inch (6-mm) squares and added to soups and stews.

Leeks: These sweet-flavored alliums look like giant green onions. Only the thick white stems and palest green parts are used. Because leeks are harvested from sandy soil, it is important to rinse out all the gritty matter that gets trapped between the many layers. To clean, trim off the dark green tops. With a sharp knife, make a deep lengthwise cut in the leek from the top to just above the root. Place the leek in a vertical position under cold running water. Then fan out all the layers and rinse well to remove any particles of dirt. Leeks are delicious in soups and make a good base for sauces.

Lemons: This versatile fruit is good in both sweet and savory dishes. While acidic in taste, lemons have an alkaline effect in the body and keep the pH of bodily fluids balanced. Freshly squeezed lemon juice can be added to fruit such as sliced apples, bananas, and avocados to prevent them from turning brown after cutting. To extract juice easily, roll lemons on the counter before cutting. This breaks up the lemon cells and releases more of the juice.

Limes: This small green citrus fruit is commonly used in Peruvian, Mexican, and Thai cuisine. It has a sour, slightly bitter taste. In hot weather, lime juice can have a cooling effect on the body. For a refreshing beverage, steep fresh mint leaves in boiled water, add some lime juice, and allow to cool. Like lemons, limes are highly acidic in taste but turn alkaline in the body. To extract juice easily, roll limes on the counter before cutting.

Maple syrup: Made from boiled-down maple tree sap, maple syrup contains a variety of minerals and is delicious in baked goods. Look for 100% pure maple syrup, not maple-flavored corn syrup. The darker the color. the deeper the maple flavor. Syrup collected early in the season has a lighter color than the syrup collected later in the season when the weather is warmer.

Marjoram: A fragrant herb belonging to the mint family, marjoram has anti-inflammatory and antimicrobial qualities. It supports respiratory health and is high in antioxidants. It is pungent, astringent, and warming according to Ayurveda. Marjoram works well as a base for soups and sauces. It can add an aromatic flavor to roasted vegetables when combined with thyme and rosemary. Although generally safe, marjoram should be avoided by pregnant and lactating women.

Millett: See Gluten-Free whole grains, page 47.

Mint: There are more than thirty varieties in the mint family, with spearmint being the most common. Fresh mint is recommended over dried mint. This herb has a refreshing, cleansing taste, and is sweet and cooling. Spearmint can be used as an herbal tea to remedy minor ailments such as headaches, fatigue, stress, or respiratory problems. To make a refreshing drink, steep fresh mint in hot water for a few minutes. Serve hot or at room temperature. Add a slice of lemon for visual appeal. The addition of freshly squeezed lime juice will further enhance mint's cooling quality.

Miso: Miso is made from fermented soybeans, rice, or barley with the addition of salt and the fungus *kojikim*. Miso has an earthy, savory flavor. It is rich in vitamins and minerals and makes a hearty base for soups, sauces, and salad dressings. Miso is high in antioxidants that help protect the body against cellular damage. As a fermented food, it can help restore beneficial bacteria in the intestinal track.

Always look for unpasteurized miso, as it has more natural enzymes. Unpasteurized miso can be used in marinades to break down vegetable fiber. There are three types of miso: white or mellow miso, yellow, and red. White miso has the mildest flavor, while red miso is intense and salty with an earthy taste. Yellow miso is somewhere in between. White miso may be used as a substitute for dairy in sauces. Red miso is perfect for hearty soups and stews and makes a tasty marinade for baked and oven-roasted vegetables, like butternut squash. As a flavoring, add just enough miso to enhance flavor, as too much can be overpowering. One or two teaspoons miso to 1 cup (8 fl oz/250 ml) boiled water is sufficient for broth. Never allow miso to boil.

Molasses: It has a distinctive sweet smoky flavor and contains iron, calcium, magnesium, and potassium. Molasses is the end product from the extraction of sugar beets or sugarcane juices. Blackstrap molasses is produced after the third boiling cycle in the sugar making process. This variety contains the least amount of sugar and has the highest concentration of vitamins and minerals. It can add flavor to sauces and marinades and can enhance the flavor of beans when 1 teaspoon to 1 tablespoon is added near the end of cooking.

Mustard seeds: These tiny round seeds are available in yellow, dark brown, and black. The yellow seeds are milder than the brown. Brown mustard seeds are commonly used in Indian dals, curries, and kitchari. These seeds are pungent and heating. You can buy them at Indian food shops as well as natural foods stores. Brown mustard seeds are the variety used in the recipes in this cookbook.

Nettle: Also referred to as "stinging nettle," it can help with detoxification to keep the body functioning optimally. It is said to promote healthy circulation, alleviate allergies, and reduce arthritic pain. Nettle can be used fresh or dried, as an extract, powder, or tincture, and taken in capsule form. Seek advice from you doctor before using nettle, as it can cause complications with certain medications and is not recommended for women during pregnancy.

Nori: Nori is a type of dried sea vegetable commonly sold in thin black sheets in packages of 10 to 12. Nori sheets make tasty gluten-free veggie wraps and are most often used to wrap sushi and California rolls. Nori can be used as a garnish on soups, salads, and vegetable dishes to add a salty sea flavor. To prepare nori for use as a garnish, toast on a baking sheet for 5 minutes in a 350° F (180° C) oven. After toasting, cut into strips or tiny squares and sprinkle on dishes before serving.

Nutmeg: A seed from a tropical tree that grows in Indonesia, nutmeg is sweet, astringent, pungent, and heating and has a pleasant aroma. Buy whole nutmeg and grate just before using for maximum flavor. In Ayurvedic holistic healing nutmeg is used to induce sleep.

Oat straw: Oat straw is most often consumed as a tea. It is available as a powder, an extract, and a supplement. This is considered the herb of longevity in Ayruveda. Other health benefits may include increased energy, improved physical performance, reduced anxiety, and lowered risk of heart disease. Those with gluten sensitivity should use with caution, as they may experience side effects.

Oats: Whole oat grains, called **groats,** take the longest to cook. **Steel-cut** oats, also called Scotch or Irish oats, are groats that have been cut in two or three places so that they will cook faster than whole groats. **Rolled oats**, sometimes referred to as "old-fashioned oats," are made from groats that have been steamed and then rolled into flakes, done to stabilize the oils they contain. They cook in less than 10 minutes, due to their greater surface area.

Quick oats are similar to rolled oats, but they have been rolled thinner and steamed longer. They have a smoother texture and cook faster than rolled. **Instant oatmeal** has been chopped fine, flattened, precooked, and hydrated. This is the most processed version of oats and often has salt and sugar added. **Oat bran** is the multi-layered skin of the edible kernels. It is rich in fiber, antioxidants, and B vitamins. See Gluten-Free Whole Grains, page 48.

Onions: See Alliums, page 58

Oregano: Popular in Italian, Greek, and Mexican cooking, oregano is astringent, pungent, and heating. It is categorized as a bitter herb. Commonly paired with tomatoes, oregano is a standard ingredient in tomato sauce.

Organic sugar: Derived from sugarcane or sugar beets that are grown and harvested according to USDA certified organic standards. Despite the organic classification, there is no difference in nutritional value between organic and conventional white sugar. The principal benefit to purchasing organic is the avoidance of pesticides and harmful chemicals.

Paprika: This spice comes from dried and ground red peppers having varying degrees of heat. The peppers used for paprika are generally milder and thinner fleshed. Originally from central Mexico, this spice was introduced to Spain in the 16th century. Paprika adds color and flavor to a variety of dishes across a range of cuisines. It can be used to stimulate digestion. Full of carotenoids, it is good for preventing night blindness and protecting the eyes from harmful ultraviolet rays.

Parsley: This fresh herb with scalloped leaves is indigenous to the Mediterranean. There are two types of parsley: curly parsley with crinkly leaves and Italian or flat-leaf parsley. It is often used in combination with thyme and bay leaves to flavor stews and soups. Parsley is a potent antioxidant, as well as an anti-inflammatory. It contains vitamins A and C and has more iron than spinach. High in vitamin K, it can support healthy bones.

Psyllium husk: This natural source of fiber, is derived from the shell of seeds of a shrub-like plant called *Plantago ovata*. The powdered form is a popular ingredient in gluten-free baking as its binding properties and elasticity produce a lighter, fluffier result. Psyllium husk can also serve as a thickener in soups and sauces. Psyllium husk is an excellent prebiotic that supports beneficial bacteria in the intestines and has been shown to relieve both constipation and diarrhea. Psyllium can be purchased in natural food stores or online in both powdered and whole husk forms. Be sure to select organic psyllium without fillers or additives. The powdered supplement form sold under the Organic India label is grown following ancient Ayurvedic practices.

Quinoa: See Gluten Free Whole Grains, page 48.

Red clover: This herb grows wild in Europe and Asia and has been cultivated to grow in North America. Red clover has a long history of use as a medicinal herb. As a blood purifier, it can gradually cleanse the bloodstream and correct deficiencies in the circulatory system. A few studies suggest that red clover can protect against heart disease and lower the risk of developing osteoporosis.

Red onions: Milder and slightly sweeter than yellow or white onions, red onions can add crunchiness and brightness to salads and salsas. These onions make a tasty side dish when cut in wedges and grilled. They work best in recipes with a short cooking time, as their flavor diminishes the longer they are cooked. Because of their deeper color, red onions have the highest phytochemical content in the allium family.

Rice vinegar: Made from fermented rice, this type of vinegar is a staple ingredient in Asian cuisine. It has a pleasant mild sweetness without the sharpness often present in other vinegars. Rice vinegar can be used to sweeten marinades and dipping sauces. It is also tasty in salad dressings and stir-fried dishes. This vinegar is high in antioxidants.

Rosemary: This aromatic herb comes from an evergreen shrub with needle-shaped leaves. Rosemary is pungent and bitter and should be used in moderation because adding too much can overpower the other flavors in a dish. It can be used fresh or dried. Because rosemary can aid in the digestion of fats and starches, it goes well with roasted potatoes.

Saffron: See Medicinal Spices, page 68.

Salt: The main purpose of salt is to add flavor to food. Ordinary table salt is the most refined with iodine and anti-caking agents added to prevent clumping. Himalayan salt is slightly lower in sodium than other salts and contains small amounts of magnesium, potassium, calcium, and iron. The presence of iron oxide in Himalayan salt gives it its pink color. Himalayan rock salt is mined in Pakistan. Sea salt comes from evaporated sea water. The darker the color the more impurities and trace minerals it will have. Sea salt may contain trace amounts of heavy metals and microscopic plastic waste. Celtic sea salt is quite moist, pale gray, and contains trace amounts of minerals. Kosher salt is a favorite with professional chefs because of its flaky texture that makes it easy to dust on food. Kosher salt is similar to table salt without the addition of anti-caking agents and iodine. The choice of salt is a personal preference. Experiment to see which works best with your cooking style. My preference is Himalayan and the salt used in the recipes in this cookbook.

Shallots: These teardrop-shaped onions are the sweetest in the allium family and are a classic ingredient in French cooking. Peeling and chopping them may require some patience, but their flavor rewards the effort. Shallots are especially flavorful as a base for soup broth and in stews.

Sun-dried tomatoes: Now popular worldwide, sun-dried tomatoes originated in southern Italy where they were sliced, dusted with salt, and dried on rooftops in the sun. High in lysopene, antioxidants, and vitamin C, sun-dried tomatoes offer significant health benefits. Their sweet-sour tartness and chewy texture make them an appealing addition to a myriad of dishes. Chopped finely, they can serve as a base for dressings and sauces. Thinly sliced sun-dried tomatoes make a tasty accent in stir-fried dishes when added during sautéing. For a yummy, easy to prepare soup, sun-dried tomatoes can be puréed with cooked seasonal vegetables in a blender. They are available in airtight bags or marinated in jars with olive oil. Unopened they keep for up to 9 months. After opening, keep refrigerated and consume within 2 weeks.

Tamari sauce: This sauce blends well with other spices and makes a good substitute for salt. It is also a quick and easy way to flavor foods. Low salt versions are available for those on a low-sodium diet. Tamari is a form of soy sauce that is gluten-free. If allergic to soy, purchase soy sauce made from coconut, generally labeled "Coco Aminos".

Thyme: An evergreen herb, thyme pairs well with bay leaves, parsley, and celery. It is an essential ingredient in herbal blends such as *bouquet garni* and *herbes de Provence* and is widely used in French and Italian cooking. Thyme complements vegetables beautifully and is good in soups, stews, and broths. Thyme is a common addition to stuffings and marinades. Be sure to add it at the beginning of cooking to allow the oils to be released.

Thyme has a long history as a culinary herb dating back to ancient Greece. Thyme is more subtle than oregano with tones of mint providing well-balanced flavor to most dishes. Fresh thyme leaves should be removed from the woody stems before use in cooking. The fresh leaves have a light, bitter, refreshing taste. Dried thyme blends well in most dishes, holding up the flavor without overpowering the food. Use with care when roasting or grilling because the dry heat tends to heighten its flavor.

Tumeric: See Medicinal Spices, page 68.

Umeboshi plums: *Ume* means "plum," and *boshi* means "to dry," although these are actually a species of apricot. This traditional Japanese condiment is a natural antibiotic that supports liver function and detoxification. It is a potent alkaline-forming food and preventative medicine that was an essential ration for samurai warriors during the feudal period in Japan.

Made by fermenting unripe plums with red shiso leaves and sea salt, umeboshi are sun-dried and aged for a year. The shiso leaves are antimicrobial, giving them an infection-fighting property. Umeboshi plums are available in 3 forms: whole plums, paste, and vinegar.

With their sour and salty taste, they can add a pleasant tartness to dressings, dips, and sauces. For a lively broth, bring a quart (liter) of water to a boil, remove from heat and add 4 umebosh plums. Soak for 5 minutes. Using a slotted spoon, transfer the plums to a cutting board and let cool to the touch. Remove the pits and mash the plums into a paste. This paste may be used as a base for a pasta sauce with olive oil and garlic. (See recipes pages 176 and 203). For a warming drink on a cold day, pour boiled water into a cup, add an umeboshi, and let stand for 2 to 3 minutes. Then drink the broth and eat the flesh of the plum.

Wakame: Popular in Asian cuisine, this green sea vegetable has a subtle sweet flavor and satiny texture. Low in calories, it has been sited as one the best food sources of iodine. Wakame is available in 2 forms: salted (sold refrigerated in a sealed package) and the dried version, which is what I use in my recipes. Wakame needs to be reconstituted before using. To do so I place it in filtered water for 5 to 10 minutes, rinse, drain, and then add to soups and stews.

White onions: Tender in texture with a thin papery skin, these onions are sharper and more pungent than yellow ones. Their high water content gives them a crispness that makes them perfect for salsas and chutneys. Sliced thinly, they are tasty on salads and sandwiches. White onions are popular in Mexican dishes and are especially delicious in *huevos rancheros* and refried beans. Select firm onions with dry skins.

White pepper: This pepper is made from peppercorns that have had their dark-colored skins removed. White pepper has a sharper flavor and is less aromatic than black. It is recommended as a substitute in white sauces and dishes that are light in color.

Yellow onions: These are a good all-purpose onion that is available year-round and most commonly used worldwide. Yellow onions are suitable for frying, roasting, and grilling. They can be used as a substitute for white or red onions in recipes. They are tasty caramelized and hold their flavor well in cooking, making them the best choice for soups, stews, and dishes that require a longer cooking time. Select firm onions with dry skins.

Bibliography

Appleton, Nancy. **Lick the Sugar Habit.** New York, NY: Avery, 2001.

Bragg, Paul and Patricia Bragg. **Healthy Heart**. Santa Barbara, CA: Health Science, 2007.

Bragg, Paul and Patricia Bragg. **The Miracle of Fasting**. Santa Barbara, CA: Health Sciences, 2004.

D'Adamo, Peter J. **Eat Right for Your Type**. New York, NY: G. P. Putman's Sons, 2002.

Diamond, Harvey and Marilyn Diamond. **Fit for Life**. New York, NY: Grand Central Publishing, 2010.

Junger, Alejandro, MD. **Clean**. San Francisco, CA: Harper One, 2012.

Lad, Usha, and Vasant Lad. **Ayurvedic Cooking for Self-Healing**. Albuquerque, NM: The Ayurvedic Press, 2002.

Ladell, Hafiz. **The Magic Cookbook: Four Directions: East**. Oxford, England: Oxford Green Print, 2006.

McKeith, Gillian. **You Are What You Eat**. London: Penguin Books Ltd, 2004.

Morningstar, Amadea. **The Ayurvedic Cookbook**. Delhi, India: Motilal Banarsdass Publishers, 2005.

Page, Melvin. **Your Body Is Your Best Doctor**. New Canaan, CT: Keats Publishing, 1976.

Palanisamy, Akil, MD. **The Paleovedic Diet**. Skyhorse Publishing, New York, NY, 2015.

Shing Ni, Mao. **The Secrets of Longevity Cookbook**. Kansas City, MO: Andrews McMeel Publishing, 2013.

Tiwari, Maya. **Ayurveda: A Life of Balance – The Complete Guide to Ayurvedic Nutrition and Body Types With Recipes.** Rochester, VT: Healing Arts Press, 1995.

Young, Robert O. and Shelley Redford. **The pH Miracle**. New York, NY: Warner Books, Inc., 2007.

Appendix

Acid-Forming Foods & Beverages

Alcoholic beverages
Animal products (meats, fish, fowl)
Breads
Cakes, muffins, bagels, pastries
Canned, glazed, sugared, and sulfured fruits
Carbonated drinks
Cereals
Chocolate, cacao
Coffee
Corn (popped, canned, frozen, processed, chips)
Crackers
Cranberries
Creamed soups and sauces
Dairy (butter, milk, cheese, yogurt, kefir)
Eggs
Fermented foods
Flour (white)
Grains (basmati, brown rice, cornmeal, oats, spelt, wheat)
Ice cream
Mustard, ketchup, pickles, most condiments
Nuts (Brazil nuts, cashews, filberts, macadamias, pecans, peanuts, pistachios, walnuts)
Nut butters
Pasta
Pomegranates
Potato chips
Rhubarb
Salt
Sugar
Tahini and seed butters
Tapioca
Tea, black
Tomatoes, cooked, and tomato sauces
Vinegar, distilled white
Wheat bran and germ

Alkaline-Forming Foods & Beverages

VEGETABLES

Artichokes
Asparagus
Black radishes
Broccoli
Brussels sprouts
Cabbage
Carrots
Cauliflower
Celery
Collard greens
Corn, fresh
Cucumbers
Daikon
Dandelion
Dulse
Garlic
Green beans
Green peas
Kale
Kelp
Kohlrabi
Kudzu root
Leafy greens
Leeks
Lettuce (except iceberg)
Mushrooms
Mustard greens
Okra
Onions
Parsley
Parsnips
Peppers (raw)
Potatoes
Pumpkin
Radishes
Rutabagas
Sea vegetables
Shiitake mushrooms
Spinach
Sprouts
Squashes
Sweet potatoes
Swiss chard
Taro
Tomatoes (raw)
Turnip greens
Turnips
Watercress
Water chestnuts

FRUITS

Apples

Avocados

Bananas (unripe)

Berries

Cantaloupe

Cherries

Currants, red

Dates

Figs

Grapefruit

Grapes

Kiwis

Lemons

Lichee nuts

Limes

Mangos

Melons

Nectarines

Passion fruit

Peaches

Persimmon

Raisins

Raspberries

Umeboshi plums

NUTS

Almonds

Coconut (fresh)

GRAINS

Amaranth

Buckwheat

Millet

Quinoa

BEANS/LEGUMES

Adzuki beans

Green lima beans

Mung beans

Soybeans

Tofu

OTHER

Apple cider vinegar

Brown rice syrup

Flaxseeds

Flaxseed oil

Ghee

Herbs

Honey, raw

Olive oil

Wheatgrass

Note: To make water more alkaline, add 1/4 teaspoon apple cider vinegar or fresh lemon or lime juice.

Products Containing Artificial Sweeteners

- Alcoholic beverages
- Baked goods
- Cereals, granola
- Chewing gum
- Condiments
- Dairy products
- Dessert toppings
- Energy bars
- Energy drinks
- Flavored syrups
- Frozen desserts
- Gelatins
- Ice cream
- Jam
- Ketchup
- Light yogurt
- Marinates
- Nutritional products
- Pie fillings
- Powdered beverage mixes
- Preserved fruits
- Puddings
- Reduced calorie fruit juice
- Salad dressings
- Sugarless candy
- Sodas
- Sweet beverages
- Table top sweeteners
- Toothpaste
- Whole wheat bread

INDEX

A

Acid-forming Foods, 16, 235. See also Balancing pH
Ajwain, 62
Alkaline-forming Foods, 16, 236-237. See also Balancing pH
Alliums, 58
Allspice, 62
Almond Butter, 88
    Almond Butter Nuggets, 121
Almonds, blanching, 219
Almond-Cardamom Macaroons, 194
Amaranth, 47
    Cream of Amaranth, 109
Antioxidants, 12
Apple Crumble, Sugarless, 192
Asparagus, Steamed, 71
Avocado Cream, Dreamy, 195
Avocado Oil, 32
Ayurveda, 10, 91, 96, 101, 142, 211
Ayurvedic
    Herbs and Spices, 56. See also Medicinal Spices
    Kitchari, 162
    Oil pulling, 18

B

Balancing pH, 16. See also Alkaline-forming Foods; Acid-forming Foods
Barley, 222
    Miso-Barley Soup, 81, 138-139
Beans. See also Chickpeas
    Black Bean Mushroom Patties, 168-169
    Cannellini Bean Hummus, 72, 124-125
    Healing Mung Bean Soup, 73, 142-143
    Make Beans More Digestible, 174
    Sweet-n-Spicy Adzuki Beans, 82, 170-171
Three-Bean Salad with Sun-Dried Tomatoes, 83, 148-149
Beets
    Beets-n-Butternut Squash, 184
    Buckwheat-Beet Pancakes, 116
    Red & Golden Beet Yogurt Salad, 71, 147
Black cumin, 63
Bouquet garnit, 55
Bread, Hearty Soda, 79, 126-127
Broccoli
    Brown Rice Pasta with Broccoli and Umeboshi Plums, 176
Buckwheat, 47
    Buckwheat-Beet Pancakes, 116
Butter, 32. See also Ghee

C

Cabbage, Red, Sesame Seed Sauté, 185
Cannellini Bean Hummus, 72, 124-125
Cardamom, 56
    Cardamom Macaroons, 74, 194
Carrots
    Carrot-Cacao Mousse, 198
    Carrot-Jicama Salad with Candied Ginger, 146
    Delicately Sweet Carrots, 187
    Kale Confetti, 78, 188
    Steamed Carrots, 70
Cauliflower, Lemon-Butter Roasted, 189
Celery
    Parsnip-Celery Soup, Puréed 78, 144
    Celery, Ghee Braised, 183
    Celery Salad with Lemon-Honey Dressing, 156
Chamomile-Fennel-Cinnamon Tea, 99. See also Teas
Chard
    Blanched Rainbow Chard with Pine Nuts, 72, 180
    Swiss Chard-Portabellos Topped with Goat Cheese, 71, 175
Chickpeas
    Chickpea & Sun-Dried Tomato Soup, Puréed, 79, 134-135
    Three-Bean Salad with Sun-Dried Tomatoes, 83, 148-149
Cilantro, 56, 223
Cinnamon, 56, 63, 224
    Cinnamon Oatmeal with Toasted Coconut, 114
    CInnamon Nuggets, Sprouted, 122
Cloves, 56, 64
Coconut-Cucumber-Cilantro Raita, 82, 210
Cold-Pressed Coffee, 105
Coriander, 56, 64
Cucumber-Mint Salad, 77, 150-151
Cumin, 56, 65. See also Medicinal Spices
Curry leaf, 56, 65

D

Dates
    Bala Breakfast, 108
    Date-Mint Chutney, 73, 211
    Sweet Spiced Lassi, 104
Detoxification, 18-19
Digestion, 20, 22
Dill, 224
    Sunflower-Dill Dressing, 205

E

Essential fatty acids, 31. See also Omega-3

F

Fennel, 54, 56, 66. See also Medicinal Spices
    Fennel-Cumin-Coriander Tea, 98
Fenugreek, 66
Fermented Foods, 13, 14, 15, 59
Flaxseeds, 31, 32, 123, 220, 237
Food preparation, 26-27
    Get Ready to Make a Recipe, 94
Friends and Food, 27

G

Garlic, 54, 58, 224
    Garlic Toast, 81
Ghee, 32, 56
    Making Ghee, 57
    Ghee Braised Celery, 183
Ginger, 15, 56, 59, 67. See also Medicinal Spices
    Ginger Herbal Tea, 96
    Ginger-Cinnamon-Cardamom Breakfast Drink, 97
    Ginger-Turmeric Sautéed Plantains, 128
    Oil-Free Lemon-Ginger Dressing, 204
Glycemic index, 16
Granola, Grain-Free Almond, Pecan, Walnut, 112-113
Green Beans
    Marinated Green Bean Red Onion Salad, 74, 154-155

H

Hemp seed oil, 32
Hemp seeds, 220
    Hemp Seed Energy Nuggets, 123
Herbal Tea, Mineralization, 102
Herbes de Provence, 55
Honey
    Celery Salad with Lemon-Honey Dressing, 156
    Honey-Dijon Mustard Dressing, 202
    Love and Support Pollinators, 218
    Raw Honey: A Mystical Universe, 214-217
Hummus, Cannellini Bean, 72, 124-125

I

Immune system, 14, 20, 101, 222

Insomnia, 101
Interviews
    From Conventional Farming to Certified Organic, 49-52
    Olive Oil, A Sacred Blessing, 34-37
    Raw Honey: A Mystical Universe, 214-217
Intestinal Health, 13, 14, 103, 104, 128
Invisible Elements in Our Food, 30

K

Kale Confetti, 78, 188
Kitchen-Efficiency, 88
Kombu, 174, 225

L

Lemons, 226
    Celery Salad with Lemon-Honey Dressing, 156
    Oil-Free Lemon-Ginger Dressing, 204
    Lemon-Butter Roasted Cauliflower, 70, 189
    Lemon-Mustard Trumpet Mushrooms with Fresh Herbs, 178-179
Lentils
    Split Red Lentils & Basmati Rice, 75, 162-163

M

Maple syrup, 226
Marjoram, 54-55, 226
Medicinal Spices, 61-68
    Ajwain, 62
    Allspice, 62
    Black Cumin, 63
    Cinnamon, 63
    Clove, 64
    Coriander, 64
    Cumin, 65
    Curry Leaf, 65
    Fennel, 66
    Fenugreek, 66
    Ginger Root, 67
    Saffron, 68
    Turmeric, 68
Microbiome, 14
Micronutrients, 145
Millet, 48
    Millet-Basmati Pilaf, 73, 158-159
Mint, 56, 226
    Mint-Cucumber Salad, 150
    Date-Mint Chutney, 73, 211
    Mint Chai, 100
    Parsley-Mint Chutney, 75, 212

Miso, 15, 59, 87, 227. See also Fermented Foods
- Baked Parsnips in Miso-Almond Butter Sauce, 186
- Miso-Barley Soup, 81, 138-139
- Miso-Vegetable Soup, 87

Molasses, 227
- Sesame-Molasses Butter Cookies, 196
- Spiced Molasses Walnuts, 129

Muffins
- Winter Squash Muffins, Spiced

Mushrooms
- Black Bean Mushroom Patties, 168-169
- Lemon-Mustard Trumpet Mushrooms with Fresh Herbs, 178-179
- Shiitake Mushroom Sauté with Leeks and Beet Greens, 76
- Shiitake Mushroom Scramble, 115
- Swiss Chard-Portabellos Topped with Goat Cheese, 71, 175

Mustard seeds, 227

N

Nettle, 228
Nori, 228
Nut Butter Sauce, 88
Nutmeg, 56, 228

O

Oat straw, 229
Oats, 48, 228-229
- Cinnamon Oatmeal with Toasted Coconut, 114

Omega-3, 31-32. See also Essential fatty acids
Oils, Purchasing and Storage Tips, 33
Olive Oil, a Sacred Blessing, 34-37
One-Dish Meals, 91
Onions, 54, 58
- Green, 58
- Red, 230
- White, 233
- Yellow, 233

Oregano 54-55, 229

P

Parsley, 55, 229
- Parsley-Mint Chutney, 75, 212

Parsnips
- Parsnip-Celery Soup, Puréed 78, 144
- Parsnips in Miso-Almond Butter Sauce, Baked, 186

Pasta
- Brown Rice Pasta with Broccoli & Umeboshi Plums, 176

    Pasta with Veggies, 90
    Spaghetti with Garlic-Basil-Tomato Sauce, 77, 160
Pecans
    Almond, Pecan, Walnut Granola, Grain-Free, 112-113
    Pecan Sun-Dried Tomato Torte wiith Garlic-Lime-Yogurt Sauce, 78, 164-165
Pesto Sauce, Pistachio, 74, 206
Plantains, Ginger-Turmeric Sautéed, 128
Playing Beat the Clock, 24-25
Pressure Cooker Meals, 92
Pumpkin-Seed Oil, 32

Q

Quick-Cooking Grains with Vegetables, 90
Quinoa Tabbouleh, 72, 152-153

R

Red Clover, 230
Rice
    Brown Rice, 47
    Brown Rice Syrup, 223
    Coconut-Cardamom Basmati Rice, Sweet, 117
    Millet-Basmati Pilaf, 73, 158-159
    Sautéed Sweet Potato, Kale & Walnuts over Brown Rice, 172-173
    Split Red Lentils and Basmati Rice, 75, 162-163
    Steamed Long-Grain Brown Rice, 83
    Steamed Short-Grain Brown Rice, 82
    Rice Cooker Combos, 91
Rice Vinegar, 230
Rosemary, 19, 54, 55, 230

S

Saffron, 56, 68, 231. See also Medicinal Spices
    Summer Saffron Paella, 80, 166-167
Sesame Seeds
    Almond Butter Nuggets, 121
    Grain-Free Almond, Pecan, Walnut Granola, 112
    Hemp Seed Energy Nuggets, 123
    Red Cabbage Sesame Seed Sauté, 185
    Sprouted Cinnamon Nuggets, 122
    Sesame-Molasses Butter Cookies, 196-197
Soup in a Blender, 86

Spinach
- Puréed Spinach Soup, 80, 136-137
- Sautéed Zucchini & Spinach with Dill, 83, 182
- Spinach with Ground Pumpkin Seed Topping, Baked, 79, 181

Spiced Milk
- Sweet Dreams, 101

Squash
- Beets-n-Butternut Squash, 184
- Roasted Zucchini with Onions and Tomatoes, 76
- Winter Squash Muffins, Spiced
- Winter Squash Soup, 140-141

Sugar, 38-45
- Alternatives to, 41, 42-43, 46
- Sources of, 44-45
- Substituting Stevia for Sugar, 42-43

Sunflower Seeds
- Savory Seed Snack, 130
- Sunflower-Dill Dressing, 205

Sweet Potatoes
- Baked Sweet Potatoes with Ghee, 78, 190
- Sautéed Sweet Potato, Kale & Walnuts over Brown Rice, 172

T
Tabbouleh. See Quinoa Tabbouleh
Teas
- Chamomile-Fennel-Cinnamon Tea, 99
- Fennel-Cumin-Coriander Tea, 98
- Ginger Herbal Tea, 96
- Mineralization Herbal Tea, 102
- Mint Chai, 100

Toaster Ovens, 92
Tofu
- Shiitake Mushroom Scramble, 76, 115

Tomatoes
- Oven-Roasted Tomatoes with Fresh Herbs, 70, 213
- Pecan Sun-Dried Tomato Torte with Garlic-Lime-Yogurt Sauce, 78, 164-165
- Tomato Sauce for All Occasions, 207

Turmeric, 68. See also Medicinal Spices
- Ginger-Turmeric Sautéed Plantains, 128

U
Umeboshi plums, 59, 232-233
- Brown Rice Pasta with Broccoli and Umeboshi Plums, 176
- Umeboshi Plum Dressing, 203

V

Vegetable Broth, 132
Vegetable Salad, Blanched, 87
Vegetable Sauté, 89
Vegetable Soup, 133
Vegetables, Steamed Seasonal, 75
Vegetables, Steamed, 89

W

Wakame, 233
Walnuts, 50
    Grain-Free Almond, Pecan, Walnut Granola, 112
    Sautéd Sweet Potato, Kale & Walnuts over brown rice, 172
    Spiced Molasses Walnuts, 129
Whole Grains, Gluten-Free, 47-48
    Keeping Grains Fresh, 48

Y

Yogurt, 15
    Plain Lassi, 103
    Red and Golden Beet Yogurt Salad, 147
    Sweet Spiced Lassi, 104

Z

Zucchini and Spinach with Dill, Sautéed, 83, 182

Acknowledgments

My gratitude to the following organizations for artist residencies that made this book possible: Dorland Mountain Arts Colony, Stonehouse Residency, and Wilbur Hot Springs. With special gratitude to the staff at the Ayurvedic Institute for suggestions and comments; Usha Lad and Dr. Vasant Lad for permission to include recipes from *Ayurvedic Cooking for Self-Healing*; Maya Twari and Healing Arts Press for permission to include recipes from *Ayurveda: A Life of Balance*; Dr. Akil Palanisamy, M.D., for reviewing the dietary recommendations; Ivy Amar and Michele Schultz for contributing recipes; Suzanne Gamache and Kendra Connor for recipe testing; Carolyn Miller and Shams Kairys for copy editing and professional advice; Annette Diniz for graphic design; Rosemary Morrison for botanical illustrations of herbs; Marcy Liston for underwriting this cookbook and continued support.

A special thank you to Mark Weiman at Regent Press for masterfully executing the design concept I envisioned for this cookbook; my writing coach, Robert Ressler for keeping me on track during challenging times; and Dr. Dina Perez-Neira for continuing support.

With much gratitude to the following friends for their encouragement and helpful suggestions Deborah D'Alesandro, Esprit Seminars; Sharon Squires and her team of friends for proof reading, Deborah Henry-Hintz, Peter Schenk. Regina Verhagen, Ritta Salastie, Johnny Henao, Linda Hough, Ineke Ebbinge, Beatrix Fife, Marki Katagiri, and all those who generously contributed.

www.ingramcontent.com/pod-product-compliance
Lightning Source LLC
Chambersburg PA
CBHW081505070526
44586CB00019B/2488